Raoul Plus, S.J.

D0028676

Winning Souls for Christ

How You Can Become an Effective Apostle

SOPHIA INSTITUTE PRESS®
Manchester, New Hampshire

Winning Souls for Christ: How You Can Become an Effective Apostle was first published in French under the title *Rayonner le Christ* (Toulouse: Editions de l'Apostolat de la Prière, 1935). In 1936, Burns, Oates, and Washbourne, London, published an English translation, titled *Radiating Christ: An Appeal to Militant Catholics*, on which this 1999 edition by Sophia Institute Press is based. In *Winning Souls for Christ*, which is published with the permission of the French Bible Association, several quotations and anecdotes from the original text have been omitted, and editorial revisions to the original English text have been made.

Copyright © 1999 French Association Biblion

All rights reserved

Printed in the United States of America

Jacket design by Lorraine Bilodeau

The cover artwork is a detail of Benozzo Gozzoli's *Adoration of the Magi*, Palazzo Medici-Riccardi, Florence Italy (photo courtesy of Archive Alinari/Giraudon).

No part of this book may be reproduced, stored in a retrieval system, or transmitted in any form, or by any means, electronic, mechanical, photocopying, or otherwise, without the prior written permission of the publisher, except by a reviewer, who may quote brief passages in a review.

Sophia Institute Press®
Box 5284, Manchester, NH 03108
1-800-888-9344
www.sophiainstitute.com

Imprimatur: John A. Floersh, Archbishop of Louisville, Kentucky
October 2, 1944

Library of Congress Cataloging-in-Publication Data

Plus, Raoul, 1882-1958.
   [Radiating Christ]
   Winning souls for Christ : how you can become an effective apostle / Raoul Plus.
      p.   cm.
   Originally published: Radiating Christ. London : Burns, Oates & Washbourne, 1936.
   Includes bibliographical references.
   ISBN 0-918477-94-8 (pbk. : alk. paper)
   1. Christian life — Catholic authors. 2. Evangelistic work. I. Title.
BX2350.2.P575 1999
248'.5 — dc21   99-13334 CIP

99 00 01 02 03 10 9 8 7 6 5 4 3 2 1

Contents

Editor's Note: The biblical references in the following pages are based on the Douay-Rheims edition of the Old and New Testaments. Where applicable, biblical quotations have been cross-referenced with the differing names and numeration in the Revised Standard Version, using the following symbol: (RSV =).

∞

*Winning Souls
for Christ*

∞

Why You Should
Be an Apostle

To be a "Christ" is the whole meaning of Christianity. To radiate Christ is the whole meaning of the Christian apostolate.

But to be a Christ for one's own personal benefit is not enough; we have to Christianize those around us — in a word, we have to radiate Christ. The following pages are intended to suggest to souls that are athirst for apostolic conquest, the means by which their apostolate may be made successful.

What method must we use in order to radiate Christ? Well, let us ask ourselves what method our Lord Himself used to gain the adherence of His contemporaries. Antecedently, it must be admitted that the means that He chose are the very means that I would do well to make my own. He, the Redeemer, possesses all the secrets of redemption. Accordingly, however His methods may astonish or even scandalize me, if I see that He chooses this formula rather than another, it is for me to submit to His judgment. His formula is certainly the good one; it must become my formula, too.

But it may be objected that Jesus Christ, the Head of the Body,[1] possessed precious resources that I, a mere member of that Body, do not possess.

---

[1] Col. 1:18.

Admittedly, Jesus possessed in His own right three qualifications that set Him entirely apart:

- He was the Son of God.
- He had at His disposal the power of miracles.
- He had a personal charm beyond compare.

But surely, continues our objector, we must lose heart from the very beginning when we consider that Jesus so far surpasses us in resources for the conquest of souls. Not at all. If we begin by contemplating what is beyond our imitation, and set our divine Head on a pedestal infinitely beyond our reach, we shall inevitably take courage. Is it not good that the Chief whom we serve is evidently and incomparably great?

And when we see how high He stands, how brightly and clearly His power shines forth, are we not filled with a boundless confidence? When Jesus says, "Be of good heart, I have overcome the world,"[2] our hearts take courage, for we see that He who leads is a Person of a different caliber from us.

He is the sort of leader with whom we can march. Under Him, victory is assured. But let us hasten to add: if Christ, our divine eldest Brother, possesses means of supernatural conquest that belong to Him alone, we must not forget that He often deigned to forego the use of these weapons, to manifest them as little as possible, and almost under protest, and that in a great number of cases, He vouchsafed to appear to His contemporaries as if He were a mere man among men, endowed with nothing more than a human power. And to that extent, the example that He has given of the manner in which we should influence others retains its full value.

---

[2] Cf. John 16:33.

But we must say more. We must say that His divine technique in the supernatural conquest of the world must be our technique too.

What did Christ do in order to win His contemporaries? The Nicene Creed tells us, and we recite the words often — perhaps without understanding that they lay upon us a greater obligation than we might think. It is all summed up in four phrases:

* He came down from Heaven;
* He became man;
* He died;
* And He was buried.

A descent, a descent from Heaven; the Incarnation; the Cross; the burial — primarily and immediately these expressions have reference only to our Lord. But, if we understand them aright, they may easily be adapted to us also, and they wonderfully describe the only true means which any savior of souls must choose if his apostolate is to be effective.

The servant is not greater than his Master.[3] Subordinate saviors cannot choose any other method than that of the principal Savior. And the rule that governs all apostolic action, all redemptive conquest, remains always that which our Lord determined. Every apostle, if his work is to be fruitful, needs a descent, or a coming down from Heaven; an incarnation; renunciation; and burial.

Our purpose is just to explain what this means. It means so many things — things that only a few people understand. And this is why there are so few genuine saviors of souls, so few

___

[3] Matt. 10:24; Luke 6:40; John 13:16.

7

people who, from God's point of view, exert real influence upon those around them.

But we may assert now from the very beginning, and as you read on, you will become more and more convinced, that any method for the salvation of souls other than that of the Savior is a fantastic creation of the imagination, an impossibility. If you are not prepared to submit to the truth, then read no further.

Part One

∞

Preparing Yourself
to Be an Apostle
for Christ

∽

Chapter One

Develop the Selflessness of an Apostle

∞

The winning of souls calls in the first place for humility: descent. The first virtue that the apostle must have if he would influence his contemporaries is disinterestedness.

What is an apostle? Etymology tells us that he is one who is sent; one who comes in the name of another; who comes not to speak of himself, not to plead his own cause, but to speak of another, to plead the cause of another — another who is understood to be greater than himself. The apostle comes to speak of God, to plead the cause of God.

In what terms does St. Paul explain the part that he and his fellow laborers are to play in the apostolate? "Separated unto the gospel,"[4] he says — set apart to preach the gospel; "dispensers of the mysteries of God";[5] and, still more briefly, God's helpers, God's fellow workers.[6] The apostles are not to preach themselves. No, not at all: it is Christ whom we preach; "for Christ we are ambassadors."[7] St. Peter's motto is the same: "If any man speak, let him speak as of the words of God."[8]

---

[4] Rom. 1:1.
[5] 1 Cor. 4:1.
[6] 1 Cor. 3:9.
[7] Cf. 1 Cor. 1:13; 2 Cor. 5:20.
[8] 1 Pet. 4:11.

And our Lord Himself, in the parable of the sower, gives us to understand that he who goes forth to sow is there to sow the seed;[9] he has to cast the seed to the four winds, seed that is not something of his own substance, but that comes from without. If you sow human seed, you will never get divine fruit — only from the divine seed will the divine plant grow. And when the good Master sends forth His Apostles to teach all nations and to baptize, He tells them that they are to do this "in the name of the Father and of the Son and of the Holy Spirit."[10] What you distribute, He says to them, distribute gratuitously, seeking no personal advantage or renown.[11]

∞

Receive God's call to spread the gospel

It is a wonderful thing that God should have made use of other men to address Himself to mankind, that He should not have contented Himself with acting within the souls of men, in the intimate recesses of their consciences. It is a wonderful thing that Christ, to awaken human beings to the truth of the gospel, should have vouchsafed to make use of "beaten air,"[12] to entrust His thought and His love to men, giving them the task of transmitting them to their brethren: "Faith, then, cometh by hearing";[13] the great majority will come to the light of truth only by making use of that instrument of Providence, the

---

[9] Matt. 13:3-8; Mark 4:3-8; Luke 8:5-8.

[10] Matt. 28:19.

[11] Cf. Matt. 5:42, 6:24.

[12] Cf. 1 Cor. 9:26.

[13] Rom. 10:17.

preacher of the gospel. "Jesus," wrote the French writer Charles Péguy, "has placed Himself at a great disadvantage; He has placed himself at the disadvantage of standing in need of us."

They will be chosen men, it is true; God will carefully select the official ministers of the Word. He will fit them by a special training for their apostolic work; they will be qualified men. The Church will have a body of teachers whose official function it will be to distribute truth — they are the priests.

Meanwhile let us not fail to pay our tribute of admiration to this wonderful creation of our Savior: the priesthood. What a difference there is between the priest and the layman! However marvelously the layman may be endowed, none of his actions can produce supernatural effects simply by means of his actions. The layman may be a channel of grace in a certain manner, by his devotion, charity, self-sacrifice, or self-denial. But what is this compared with the power of the priest, who by Baptism can make God enter into the soul, and by Penance restore Him; compared with the power of the priest at the bedside of the dying? The layman may help to prepare a soul for grace, but he cannot confer it. The layman may help to dispose a soul for pardon, but only the priest can grant absolution.

This is not to say that the priest alone is commanded to be an apostle. No, the laity also — especially in the present day, when vocations to the priesthood are so few — are called to work for the salvation of their brethren.

∞

Point to Christ, not to yourself
What qualities do the laity need especially for this work? In the first place, they need the deep humility of the man who

seeks not to publish himself, but strives to disappear entirely behind the One whom he wants to preach.

Look at St. John the Baptist. Men came to seek him, thinking that perhaps he was the Messiah. No. He, John the Baptist, was not worthy even to loosen the sandals of the Master and Savior.[14] "See," he said, "there is the Messiah." And he pointed to a man clad in a burnoose, who came forth from the desert. It is to Him that he sent his hearers and his disciples: "He must increase, but I must decrease":[15] a wonderful example of disinterestedness.

Andrew had been privileged to approach the Lord; he told his brother Simon: "We have seen the Messiah."[16] He did not add: "You need not go to Him; I will tell you all about Him." No, he invited Simon to come in person and see the Master: "He brought him to Jesus."[17]

It is not for the intermediary to seek his own advantage and glory. It is his duty to show the way to the Master — and then to disappear.

Look at St. Paul. What is his aim? To make Christ reach the measure of the perfect man,[18] by gathering together as many disciples as possible for the Savior, and by leading them to the highest possible degree of evangelical perfection. And what part does St. Paul ask for himself in this enterprise? Work? Yes, decidedly. Glory? Not at all. "I judged not myself to

---

[14] Mark 1:7; Luke 3:16; John 1:27.

[15] John 3:30.

[16] John 1:41.

[17] John 1:42.

[18] Cf. Eph. 4:13.

know anything among you, but Jesus Christ."[19] Paul is nothing. It is Jesus only who counts.

And better still, we have the magnificent example of our Lord Himself, who shows us how disinterestedness can win souls.

What does the Savior seek? He seeks to win love for His Father. For Him that is everything; He wants nothing else. It is always of the Father that He speaks. His mission is to speak to the world the words that the Father has committed to Him to speak to the world: "The Father is greater than I. . . . The words that I speak to you, I speak not of myself."[20] "He that sent me is with me; and He hath not left me alone. For I do always the things that please Him. . . . I came not of myself, but He sent me."[21] And when the Apostles ask Him to teach them how to pray, our Lord teaches them the Our Father.[22]

Hence the first condition of an effective apostolate is to work, not for oneself, but for God, for Christ. But working for God, for Christ, may be understood in a thousand ways. The only good way is to love the cause you have espoused, and to love it with all your heart.

∞

Be zealous

Zeal, if it is to be truly zeal, must be a passion, a noble sort of jealousy; a zeal of flame and fire. We must hunger and thirst

[19] 1 Cor. 2:2.
[20] John 14:28, 10.
[21] John 8:29, 42.
[22] Luke 11:1-4.

for justice;[23] we must be tormented at the thought of those who suffer: "I have compassion on the multitude."[24] We must not have a compassion that is mere sentiment, mere words, but one that is active, genuine, and therefore effective. "Not in word nor in tongue, but in deed and in truth."[25]

When souls appreciate that he who wishes them well is, in the first place, absolutely disinterested, and second, is desirous of their perfection, then they allow themselves to be approached; they are won by warmth as a warm stream melts an iceberg. Anything else can be resisted; but you cannot resist a burning zeal, if that zeal, as we have said, is disinterested, and if it is, as we shall say later, enlightened.

Who can measure the good that was done, for example, through the ardent charity of a Pierre Poyet or an Antoine Martel. Poyet, unable to convert one of his companions, wrote: "Christ seemed to say to me this morning: 'It depends solely upon you whether this soul will be saved, whether it will believe in me and love me. Will your faith and your love be great enough to win it?' I trembled with terror before this responsibility: the salvation of a soul."

Antoine Martel, a brilliant graduate, professor of Slavonic literature at the University of Lille, in a paper on the subject of "Charity and the Professional Virtues," wrote as follows:

"To live charity means, above all, to have the spirit of service, the spirit that makes us ready to spare others pain and render them service, even though it may cost us a part of our

---

[23] Matt. 5:6.
[24] Matt. 15:32; Mark 8:2.
[25] 1 John 3:18.

own resources — money, time, health, intelligence, powers of action. We are one of God's hands: the hand that works from without, while the other acts from within. We can, to a great extent, remove from the hearts of our brethren that which obstructs their approach to God. The only thing that can deliver us from our obstinate human illusions is a long exposure of our hearts to the truths of the gospel."

He reproaches himself with having to write on charity, instead of living it. And yet what love he showed for his brethren! He wanted to go back to Russia, where he had already been for purposes of study. What drew him to return? Was it curiosity, the desire for learning? Above all it was "sympathy in the best sense of the word, the desire to suffer with those whose suffering he well understood."

"I feel this great people suffering," he wrote, "and I think I should rejoice to share its unhappiness, to endure willingly the evils which it is forced to bear. It is this, rather than the feeling that I should be able to bring them any help or comfort. . . . This desire to share the suffering of one who is in distress may include that desire for suffering which so many saintly souls have had, simply because they knew that their beloved, our Lord, had undergone martyrdom, that He continued to suffer in His Mystical Body, that He was 'in agony until the end of the world.' Is this not a supreme proof of love?"[26]

In this passage, Martel touches upon the ultimate reasons for devoting oneself to the salvation of souls. We must love souls for three reasons especially: because every soul represents some (perhaps much) fruit of the Blood of Christ; because

[26] Antoine Martel, *Lettres, Edition du Cerf,* 172.

every soul is a factor (perhaps a very important one) in the coming of the kingdom of God; and because in doing good to a soul, we do good to Christ in His Mystical Body.

∽

Be convinced of the truth you preach

If it is truly not his own cause that he is pleading, but God's, then the apostle will assert that truth with calmness, precisely because he is sure of the truth which he preaches, because he is in firm and conscious possession of the formula of salvation. And nothing is more convincing than the apostle's calm and uncompromising manner, his tranquil assurance, that absence of prevarication and inconsistency: thus it is, and not otherwise. And whatever you do or say, not one iota will he change:[27] "Let your speech be yea, yea; no, no."[28] What is, is; what is not, is not.

In this our Lord was our great model. We like people to assert; we like people who give the impression of sureness, so that if they say anything, it means that this is so, and they will not go back upon it. There are so many who use shifts and evasions, trying to convey the impression of subtlety, while really uncertain of themselves. You will not win adherents by cleverness — you may gain a concession, but you will not win admiration.

Even when Jesus saw that He offended His hearers, He persisted in His statements. His message, the good tidings, came from above. Whatever happened, He would transmit that

[27] Cf. Matt. 5:18.
[28] Matt. 5:37.

message intact. And the world likes it so, even though it may protest and refuse to submit.

Many of the teachings of the Savior ran counter to the current opinions of the time; whether it was a question of the requirements of charity, the forgiveness of injuries, or the pardon accorded to repentance, whether it was a question of the predominance of the internal motive over the soulless practice of external rites, or the danger of riches, or the pharisaical spirit, our Lord never attenuated His doctrine. It was the same in the matter of the Real Presence, the eternity of the pains of Hell, and the doctrine of the straight way, and the narrow gate.[29] "This saying is hard," said many of His hearers, and they went away.[30] But see, on the other hand, the confidence of those who remained faithful; see how, when the hour came, they gave evidence of their attachment to this Master of unparalleled assurance, even by the shedding of their blood.

And St. Paul, following the example of his Master, knew how to be assertive when it was necessary. He had been accused of appealing to the resurrection of the dead, and on that account he was cited to appear before the Jewish council. Did he attempt to evade the issue? On the contrary, he faced it: "Men, brethren . . . concerning the hope and resurrection of the dead, I am called in question."[31] And his frankness, far from resulting in his downfall, gained him the favor of the multitude: "We find no evil in this man!"[32]

[29] Matt. 7:13; Luke 13:24.
[30] John 6:61 (RSV = John 6:60).
[31] Acts 23:6.
[32] Acts 23:9.

Young people especially like courage. A young naval ensign had lost his rosary. "To whom does this thing belong?" asked a comrade who had found it. "To me," replied the owner. Did they jeer at him? Did he lose anything in their esteem? On the contrary, he became thenceforth the refuge of any of his comrades who happened to be in trouble.

Nobody admires the half-hearted giver. Our Lord did not. A judicious mixture of courage and cowardice is odious; what is neither hot nor cold, but tepid, He vomits out of His mouth.[33]

"There is no giving in to evil," wrote dramatist Paul Claudel, "there is no giving in to deceit. There is only one thing to do with what is evil, and that is to destroy it." And Alfred Vigny wrote: "Any man who has ideas and does not form them into a complete system is an incomplete man." And the German poet and playwright Johann Goethe said, more briefly still: "If you have seen a man who is a complete whole, you have seen a great thing."

People like to see men who are, as they say, of one piece, that is, consistent. Why are such men so rare? In the case of many of the baptized, to use the cruel saying of the German poet Heinrich Heine, "the waters of Baptism dry quickly." What a pity, and what a shame! How many there are who act as though one or other part of their being had not been touched by the sacred waters! But what a joy, on the contrary, to find a person who is truly one, fully logical and consistent, in whom all is marked with the baptismal seal!

"Are you a member of the sacred band? Are you a follower of Christ?" I can imagine two answers, one of them, the bold,

---

[33] Rev. 3:16.

courageous reply: "Yes, of course I am!"; and the other, the answer of the coward: "Well, you see how it is; somebody persuaded me, and I did not want to refuse."

We are familiar with this second reply: does it not recall the answer of a certain apostle, when he was accosted by a servant girl, on the night of our Lord's arrest: " 'Thou also wast with Jesus the Galilean.' But he denied before them all, saying: 'I know not what thou sayest.' "[34] Which of the two attitudes, the courageous or the evasive, is the more to be admired?

We may remark also that when Christ asserts His identity, He makes no compromise: " 'Art Thou the Christ, the Son of the blessed God?' 'I am.' "[35] "I am"; nothing more — that is enough. "You call me Master and Lord. And you say well, for so I am."[36]

The apostle must imitate the Master. But in his uncompromising firmness, if it is to be convincing, there must enter no element of self. It is not the person who speaks, but what is said, that matters.

[34] Cf. Matt. 26:69-70.
[35] Mark 14:61-62.
[36] John 13:13.

Chapter Two

∞

Work with Others
for God's Glory

∞

While firmness on principles must be absolute, adaptiveness to individuals should be cultivated to the utmost. Our Lord gave Himself to all: to children; to sinners (Mary Magdalene, Simon, those possessed by devils[37]); to the timid (Nicodemus[38]); to the discouraged (the disciples of Emmaus[39]); to condemned criminals (the thief on the cross[40]). He showed no preferences, unless it was for the most distressed. He took the lost sheep upon His shoulders. He adapted Himself to all. It was in imitation of this model that St. Paul became all things to all men that he might win them to Christ.[41] The good Master did not crush the broken reed, nor did He extinguish the smoking flax.[42] When questions were put, He answered them; when they asked Him how to pray, He taught them.

Indeed, you might say that our Lord did nothing else but place Himself at the disposal of any who wished to ask Him a question or a favor. He never seemed to be in a hurry. It is

---

[37] Mark 16:9; Matt. 26:6, 8:16.
[38] John 3:1-5.
[39] Luke 24:15, 25-31.
[40] Luke 23:39-43.
[41] 1 Cor. 9:22.
[42] Matt. 12:20.

difficult to open your heart to one who appears always to be preoccupied or busy. "Seeing the multitudes, He went up into a mountain. And when He was seated, His disciples came unto him."[43] On another occasion: "Jesus, going out of the house, sat by the seaside. . . . He went up into a boat and sat."[44] "On a certain day . . . He sat teaching."[45]

∽

Be welcoming and attentive

What a lesson for us! Sitting down was equivalent to saying: "See, I am at your disposal, I am entirely at your service. I am most interested in what you have to say to me." Georges Duhamel once wrote: "The majority of people seem to suffer from a sense of neglect; they are unhappy because nobody takes them in hand, nobody is ready to accept the confidences they offer." And Ernest Hello wrote, more briefly: "The great glory of charity is to understand."

That is what is needed — the gift of understanding others, the spontaneous offer of help; engaging a person in conversation on indifferent matters for a few minutes, just to give him the chance to say what he wants to say but does not dare.

René Bazin somewhere speaks of a peasant he knew who, every morning, used to go out into the fields and listen to the corn growing.

In the same way, we ought to be able to listen to the seed that is growing in men's hearts, help it to sprout, break up the

---

[43] Cf. Matt. 5:1.
[44] Matt. 13:1-2.
[45] Luke 5:17.

clod of earth that the seed is too feeble to penetrate; and signify by a pressure of the hand, a smile, or a passing word, that we are at the service of another, ready to welcome him, to give him our attention, to help — in a word, to devote ourselves to him.

∞

Don't try to do everything yourself

You may be defending God's cause, but remember that you are not its only champion. You must not try to do everything by yourself; and this is another way of practicing that disinterestedness that is so effective a weapon in the hands of the apostle.

If there was ever one who might have accomplished unaided the whole task of redemption, surely it was our Lord. What need had He of help? And yet, with an unparalleled humility, He chose fellow workers, He gathered His disciples around Him, not to pay court to Him, but because He wanted to ask of them this curious service: to help Him, the Master of the world, to save the world.

Often, instead of going Himself to preach the word or to do good, He sent His disciples in His place. They would do as well as He; indeed, sometimes, with His permission, they would do better. He promised it in so many words: "He that believeth in me, the works that I do, he also shall do; and greater than these shall he do."[46] Indeed, He pushed His disinterestedness so far as to accept failure for Himself, allowing another to carry His program into effect. He, Jesus, did not "succeed" — He

[46] John 14:12.

died crucified, defeated, with all His Apostles in flight. The Holy Spirit had to come to begin the evangelical conquest of the world.

The application to our own case is easy. We must submit to being assisted by others, and not make ourselves the sole center of beneficent activity; we must choose collaborators, give them work to do; we must be pleased to see them succeed, and even be pleased to see them succeed better than ourselves. Nothing is more admirable than such selflessness, perhaps because it is so difficult — and so rare.

∞

Build on the apostolic work of others

It is an attractive form of self-denial to admit others to work with you; you should welcome others to work by your side — that is, you should be pleased to have other forms of apostolic activity besides that form which you yourself favor. But also, you should be prepared to admit that there has been devoted work done *before* your time, work that has not been without fruit.

The young are especially inclined — so wrapped up are they in their own form of apostolate — to be resentful or critical of those who do not share their own particular type of work. The scout will think that there is nothing like scouts; the XYZ organization will think that there is nothing like the XYZs, forgetting that in the Father's house "there are many mansions."[47] Others are wont to imagine that before their time nothing was ever done.

[47] John 14:2.

Did our Lord despise the past? Far from it; He did not deny the value of the Old Testament, although it was His task to found the New. He often appealed to it, He often quoted the prophets. "I am not come to destroy," He said, "but to fulfill."[48] Let this be our motto. Admittedly a new situation requires treatment; of course it is easy, in one's enthusiasm for one type of work, to overlook the advantages of an earlier — or a neighboring — organization. But such narrowness of outlook runs the risk of antagonizing others.

The apostle's soul has a vaster vision. He is enthusiastic for his own organization and his own methods, but he is able, at the same time, to recognize the advantages of the organizations that have existed in the past and that still exist today, side by side with his own. A passionate zeal is a conquering force, but only if it is broad-minded. A narrow mind or a narrow heart will never conquer others.

∞

Work constantly for Christ

The apostle is in the service of Christ. But what sort of service is it? Is it a casual employment, a sporadic service, with intervals during which everything is left to go to rack and ruin — or a constant service that takes up every minute of our time?

Are there any holidays in the service of Christ? In other words, are there certain moments when the blood of Christ is inoperative, when the Redemption is without effect? Surely, the kingdom of God calls for help at every moment; souls are

---

[48] Matt. 5:17.

constantly in need of our aid; incessantly the blood of Christ cries to Heaven.

You are not an apostle for only half an hour a day, during the period of a meeting, or under certain circumstances — you are an apostle all the time, for twenty-four hours a day, for sixty minutes an hour, for sixty seconds a minute. The apostolate is the work of every moment; not always of the same sort at every moment, but the work of every moment.

Again, consider the example of our Lord. Not for a moment did He forget the purpose for which He came. Whether in the synagogue or in the Temple, in the boat or on the shore, conversing with the Samaritan woman[49] or appearing before Pilate, with His Apostles, or before His judges — He is filled always with the sense of His mission. "My Father worketh until now; and I work."[50] Christ worked incessantly. The great task of the salvation of the world is a continuous drama, without intervals. The sentence we have just read was uttered by our Lord in answer to the Pharisees who had accused Him of healing the sick on the Sabbath.

Every instant God gives us being and life, and at every instant grace presses us.[51] Every instant, souls stand in need of us; every instant, the Father wants us to glorify Him; every instant, the Son asks us to help Him.

"Every day, they ceased not . . . to teach and preach Christ Jesus."[52] So we are told of the Apostles in the early days of the

---

[49] John 4:7-26.
[50] John 5:17.
[51] Cf. 2 Cor. 5:14.
[52] Acts 5:42.

Church. The rule is still the same and equally urgent. The occasion will not always call for the same sort of activity; there is an apostolate for the time of work, and an apostolate for the holidays. But there is no holiday from the apostolate. The Father works without ceasing; so did Christ; so does the Holy Spirit within the souls of men, calling them and assisting them at every moment, although they may not know it. So did the Twelve; not a day passed without their preaching Christ. And so do all apostles who understand the meaning of their vocation. "All the time, and with all my soul" is the apostle's motto.

The primary rule for every apostle is that he must be willing to disappear behind the Master whom he preaches. We should add that the apostle must devote himself to humble tasks; he must be able, as they say, "to descend to details"; he must not be content merely to have great ideas; he must come down to the concrete and attend to humble realities.

And Christ, the greatest of all leaders, never disdains the smallest trifles: those slow advances and that patient attention to detail necessary to overcome obstacles apparently insignificant, but in reality of the highest importance.

∞

Be all things to all people

See the care with which He chooses and prepares His Apostles. Consider how carefully He studies the method of approach to be used for different individuals! Recall the episode with Nicodemus, with the woman of Samaria, with the centurion whose servant was sick.[53] There is no place or opportunity

---

[53] Matt. 8:5-13; Luke 7:2-10.

that the Savior does not utilize. He converses as easily with Zacchaeus in the sycamore tree as with Nathanael under the fig tree;[54] with Simon the Pharisee in his dining room as with the Samaritan woman by the side of the well; with the masters of Israel in the synagogue as with the paralytic under the portico of the pool of Probatica.[55]

And how wonderfully He adapts His method to the character of those with whom He speaks! Sometimes it will be a question that He puts to obtain the answer He desires: " 'Whom do men say that I am?' 'Some, John the Baptist, and others, Elijah, and others, Jeremiah or one of the prophets.' . . . 'But who do you say that I am?' . . . 'Thou art Christ, the Son of the living God.' "[56]

At other times it is a sentence that arouses curiosity, a paradox: "I am come not to bring peace but the sword."[57] "He that would save his life shall lose it."[58] "If thy right hand scandalize thee, cut it off."[59] "Whatsoever thou shalt bind upon earth, it shall be bound also in Heaven."[60] "Whither I go you cannot come."[61]

Sometimes, although rarely, there is a sudden outburst, in order to impress a lesson more deeply upon the minds of His

[54] Luke 19:2-6; John 1:47-49.
[55] Cf. Matt. 13:54; Mark 6:2; John 5:5-9.
[56] Matt. 16:13-16.
[57] Cf. Matt. 10:34.
[58] Cf. Matt. 16:25.
[59] Matt. 5:30; Mark 9:42 (RSV = Mark 9:43).
[60] Matt. 16:19.
[61] John 8:21, 13:33.

hearers. The Temple of God is to be respected, and so He drives out the sellers with scourges. Thus His hearers will remember the lesson: "My house is the house of prayer."[62] Similarly, when He wants to confound hypocrisy: "You whited sepulchers!"[63]

But ordinarily Christ's voice is calm and measured. He speaks in simple and homely fashion. Sometimes His voice is stern. But at all times He adapts Himself to His audience.

Jesus is not only at His ease with children, with the Twelve, with His own friends, Martha, Mary, Lazarus,[64] and certain of His disciples. He speaks to everybody, as He meets them, be they officials, judges, or adversaries — to every age and condition of men. He puts Himself within the reach of all. He says what has to be said at the moment, awaiting God's own time to say what remains to be said. "You cannot bear it now."[65] "He that hath ears to hear, let him hear."[66] He will return to the subject later if need arises, and if circumstances permit; if necessary He will create those circumstances, provided His hearers show their goodwill, and do not insist upon remaining deaf to His words.

When He knows that a particular doctrine is beyond the capacity of the masses, our Lord asks His chosen ones to keep it to themselves for the present. To what purpose is it — in His own singularly forcible words — to place pearls before

---

[62] Luke 19:46.

[63] Matt. 23:27.

[64] John 11:5.

[65] Cf. John 16:12.

[66] Matt. 11:15; Mark 4:9; Luke 8:8.

swine?[67] Everything is not meant for all in the same degree, nor for all at the same time. The graces of one are not the graces of another, and "in the house of the Father there are many mansions."

∞

Do good works for God's glory, not your own

When He achieves a notable success, or works a particularly striking miracle, our Lord attributes all glory to God, without whom man cannot add to his stature one cubit.[68] "Seek ye first the kingdom of God."[69] Then He effaces Himself, or asks the beneficiary to disappear.

After He has raised to life the twelve-year-old daughter of Jairus, a leader of the synagogue, our Lord forbids the parents to tell anyone about the miracle.[70] After healing two blind men, He warns them, "See that no man knows this."[71] After healing the leper, He charges him that he should tell no man.[72] And after healing the man with the withered hand and other sick persons, He charges them that they should not make Him known.[73] After the multiplication of the loaves, He Himself disappears to escape the ovations of the crowd.[74]

---

[67] Matt. 7:6.

[68] Matt. 6:27; Luke 12:25.

[69] Matt. 6:33.

[70] Mark 5:43; Luke 8:56.

[71] Matt. 9:30.

[72] Luke 5:14.

[73] Matt. 12:16.

[74] John 6:15.

What He Himself practiced on the occasion of His successes He bids us do in the case of any good work: "When thou dost an almsdeed, sound not a trumpet before thee, as the hypocrites do in the synagogues and in the streets, that they may be honored by men. . . . And when thou dost alms, let not thy left hand know what thy right hand doth, so that thy alms may be in secret; and thy Father who seeth in secret will repay thee. And when thou pray, thou shalt not be as the hypocrites that love to stand and pray in the synagogues and corners of the streets, that they may be seen by men. . . . But thou, when thou shalt pray, enter to thy Father in secret. . . . When thou fastest, anoint thy head and wash thy face, that thou appear not to men to fast, but to thy Father who is in secret."[75]

Here are two precious lessons, therefore, from which we may derive singular profit: on the one hand, a wise and patient application to detail, sedulous attention to humble but important realities, and a careful choice of the best method of approach to individual souls; and on the other hand, when our efforts are crowned with success, a desire to remain hidden, and a horror of bluff and ostentation.

[75] Matt. 6:2-6, 17-18.

Chapter Three

Seek Close Union with Christ

∞

What is it that we want to communicate to our brethren? Something human? No. Something divine. And how are we to do this unless we are already, as far as possible, reservoirs of divine force? The ABC of all supernatural work is that every apostle must be an instrument united to God.

The talents and intelligence that bring success, the psychological insight that ensures delicacy and tact, the vivacity that attracts, the fine assurance that knows no timidity, the power of initiative, and the rest — all these may carry conviction. But if they are not supported by an immense reserve of divine force, the apostolate will soon stop short. You may labor much, but you will achieve nothing. There will be plenty of outward fuss, but no serious work will be accomplished. It will be a human scaffolding, to collapse with the first breath of wind.

The first, and obligatory, means of union with God — essential union with God — is the state of grace.

What would happen if you passed milk through a coal sack? How much whiteness would remain after the experiment? The more pronounced the personal imperfections of an apostle are — selfishness, egoism, the spirit of criticism, pride, impurity — the more the graces of God will be adulterated, spoiled, and attenuated as he attempts to transmit them to others.

From this point of view, the apostolate of the laity calls for greater sanctity than that of the priest. Admittedly, by reason of the unparalleled dignity that he has received, the priest is bound to strive after the highest possible degree of holiness. But his sanctity does not affect the *opus operatum* ("the act done") when he administers the sacraments. In other words, the validity of the sacrament is — by a great mercy of God — independent of the sanctity of the minister. If the minister is holy, so much the better — he will add something to the effect of the sacrament. But the validity and efficacy of the sacrament as such is not conditioned by the holiness of him that administers it.

The layman, on the other hand, being unable to administer grace through the sacraments, can make use only of the *opus operantis* ("the act of the doer") — that is to say, of his own virtue and power. And if, when he is doing his apostolic work, he is lacking in the essential degree of virtue, if he is not in the state of grace, what can he give to the world but empty words and meaningless gestures? How can he create life when he himself is a corpse? A lay apostle who is not himself alive with the life of God, or at any rate striving to live that life, is a useless cog in the machinery.

"The time is past," wrote novelist François Mauriac, "when men could profess principles at variance with their conduct. How many there were who used to try to reconcile the love of Catholicism with the anarchy of the soul! Our salvation lies in the fact that young people have now come to understand what is required of them in the secret recesses of their hearts, if their public life is to bear fruit." And this is true not only of the present day; it is true of a fruitful apostolate for all time.

∞

Draw close to God

But the state of grace is not enough. The state of grace means that the apostle is not a bad instrument. But there are many ways of being a good instrument. An instrument may serve sufficiently, and it may serve perfectly — and there are many intermediate degrees. The best workman, the best channel of the divine, is the one who is nearest to God, most conformable to His will, and closest to His heart.

In a moving essay entitled "Working with God," P. L. de Grandmaison wrote: "It is a recognized fact that pure souls radiate purity around them, inspire good thoughts, and exclude bad ones. They act like a 'sacrament' — minus, of course, the grace that comes *ex opere operato*, and observing all due proportion and respect. 'God is there,' you feel like saying when you approach a Stanislaus Kostka, a John Berchmans, an Aloysius of Gonzaga, a Rose of Lima, or a Catherine of Siena.[76] It is especially children and sinners (if these last are touched by God's grace) who feel this influence, because they are especially in tune — or if out of tune, they regret being out of tune — with pure souls.

∞

Prepare for your apostolate with quiet prayer

And so we are confronted with the question: What degree of union with God must the apostle possess? And since union

---

[76] St. Stanislaus Kostka (1550-1568), Jesuit novice; St. John Berchmans (1599-1621) and St. Aloysius Gonzaga (1568-1591), Jesuit priests; St. Rose of Lima (1586-1617) and St. Catherine of Siena (c. 1347-1380), Dominican Tertiaries.

with God is the fruit of recollection, the effect of the spirit and life of prayer, how prayerful must the apostle be?

Our model here must be again — and always — our Lord, whether it be a question of recollection and prayer before action, or during action itself.

How did our Lord act before beginning the preaching of His gospel? He prayed and lived a life of recollection for thirty years. What a lesson for us, who are always wanting to get there before we start, who, having only the tiniest stock-in-trade, are anxious to give out what little we have as soon as we can, and thus become bankrupt!

Now our Lord is about to start work. He is thirty years of age; the time has come. Shall we hear Him now? No, not yet. He goes off into the desert for forty days.[77] He wishes His words to rest upon the support of silence; and in the desert, far from all noise and contact with men, He recollects Himself. Does He need it? Not at all; but He wants to set an example for us.

And how many of us are going to profit by it? We are ready to move, act, and make a great fuss. But how many of us are capable of kneeling quietly, leaving the world alone for a while? How many of us can force ourselves to be in solitude with the Master for any length of time? How many of us estimate retreats and times of recollection at their true value?

Few, I fear! And that is why an apostolate is so often ineffective. Apostolic energy is not lacking, but the apostolic energy lacks preparatory recollection. There has not been enough prayer before action. There has not been enough speaking *to* God before speaking *about* God; or rather, there has not

[77] Matt. 4:1-2; Mark 1:12-13; Luke 4:1-2.

been enough listening to God, who wants to communicate Himself to the soul and to fill it.

Moses wants to move his people. He speaks to them, and they will not listen. Then Moses leaves the plains, departs from the multitude. He leaves his people, not because he intends to abandon them, but because he wants to be of greater service to them. He ascends the heights of Mount Sinai, takes off his shoes, and, on the lonely heights, seeks contact with God. He recollects himself, listens, and prays.

When he comes down from the mountain, he is no longer the same Moses. In his hands he has the true words that he has to say — not the words that he himself had invented, but the words that the Lord had dictated to him. He has around his head a light that will manifest his power — a reflection of his conversation alone with God. He has seen the invisible One, as the Bible puts it, and when the Hebrews receive him, they recognize beyond all doubt that God has spoken to their leader. Moses has won the day. He casts down the golden calf,[78] and the people offer no resistance; they listen to him. Again, across the desert they follow him toward the Promised Land, in spite of hunger, thirst, serpents — in spite of all.

It was the same with the apostle Paul. See him now, converted, burning with zeal, his mind made up to preach the Jesus whose disciples he has persecuted until now. Doubtless he will set forth without delay, going from city to city, preaching, baptizing, and making converts. But no, he crosses the Jordan and takes the sandy path that leads to the heart of the Arabian desert, and there he dwells. For how long, do you

[78] Exod. 34:29-35; 32:15-20.

think? For a few days, a few weeks? The world is waiting for him to begin his missionary journeys, yet Paul remains in the desert for three years.[79]

The twelve Apostles, on the eve of the Ascension, received the command from our Lord to preach the gospel to the world.[80] Surely, as soon as their Master had disappeared from sight, they would set out for the four corners of the earth. Yet, see how they shut themselves up in the supper room and remain there for nine days in prayer and recollection. "They were all persevering in prayer with Mary, the Mother of Jesus."[81] It is only after this period, when the Holy Spirit had descended upon them, that they went forth "to set the world on fire."[82]

What a curious conception we have of the apostolate, and of the method of winning souls! How different from the methods of Jesus, of Moses, of Paul! And yet we are surprised to find that our apostolate bears no fruit, that we fail to impress our contemporaries. Whose fault is it?

The most essential preliminary condition for all fruitful missionary work is silent prayer. The world does not need men who are active as much as it needs men who are ready to sacrifice their impetuosity in order to make their activity fruitful by prayer.

"When man has nothing better to do, he thinks," said a humorist. What a pity! It is bad enough when this is said of the ordinary person; but the apostle of whom this can be said truly

---

[79] Gal. 1:17-18.
[80] Mark 16:15.
[81] Acts 1:14.
[82] Cf. Luke 12:49.

is no apostle at all. Thought, recollection, and prayer should be our first preoccupation.

If we only realized how much our Lord wants us to be near Him, so that in the quietness of prayer, He may communicate to us the secret of the conversion of the world! It is a remarkable thing that while the Apostles dared only call themselves servants, Jesus calls them by the name of "friends."[83] Peter calls himself "servant and apostle of Jesus Christ";[84] James, "the servant of God and of our Lord Jesus Christ."[85] Jesus Himself calls them "children."[86] He is always anxious to have them near Him. "He made that twelve should be with him."[87] And we often read in the Gospels: "The twelve were with him."[88]

The Apostles are at Cana,[89] in the house of Simon the Pharisee; they are present at the miracles and the preaching of Christ. They will never leave Him for long. When our Lord rests at the well of Jacob, they quickly return from the town. "For his disciples were gone. . . . And immediately His disciples came."[90] St. Luke represents our Lord as praying alone; but then he adds: "As He was alone praying, His disciples also were with Him."[91] They are present at the scene of the sellers

---

[83] John 15:15.
[84] 2 Pet. 1:1.
[85] James 1:1.
[86] Mark 10:24.
[87] Mark 3:14.
[88] Luke 8:1.
[89] John 2:1-2.
[90] John 4:8, 27.
[91] Luke 9:18.

in the Temple, the blessing of the children, at the agony (although unhappily at a distance), and at the Ascension.[92]

Often when He had spoken to the multitude, our Lord turned and addressed a few words to them alone. Thus, after the promise of the Eucharist, when many of His hearers had left Him, refusing to believe, He said to His disciples: "Will you also go away?"[93] The longest discourse our Lord ever delivered was that to His Apostles (only eleven now, alas!) after the Last Supper.[94]

The Master desired always to have His Apostles by His side, and the Apostles desired always to be with their Master. Of these two desires, the first assuredly remains undiminished. But what of our desire to be close to the Master as continually as possible? We have as much time as we want for the distractions and occupations of the world, but it seems that for a heart-to-heart talk with God, we cannot find a minute.

Silence — I mean that prayerful silence that Fr. Frederick Faber calls "an eighth sacrament" — is the source of all fertility, the father of all words and all actions that are not vain. Supernatural expansion is the child of intense concentration, the child of prayer. Words and activity are an expenditure of energy; silence and prayer are its source. The brightness of the stars is seen only at night. Happy are those who believe that they are not wasting their time when they escape from the glaring publicity of the day, and dare to stand face-to-face with

---

[92] Mark 11:15-26; Matt. 19:13, 26:36-37; Mark 16:19; Luke 24:51; Acts 1:9.

[93] John 6:68 (RSV = John 6:67).

[94] John 13:31-16:33.

solitude. It is then that Heaven appears. And how are we to speak of Heaven if we have never "seen" it?

That we should pray before acting is a rule that holds not only for important and vital decisions. It is a rule for every day. For the apostle, there should never be a single day that does not include some time set apart for recollection before God. This habit of constraining oneself to devote a particular time every day to prayer will engender the habit of spontaneous prayer. We shall pray almost at every moment, and especially when we are called upon to take some important action, especially an action that concerns our neighbor.

We often read in the Gospel that our Lord, before beginning some very important action, recollects Himself and raises His eyes to Heaven. Again and again He goes apart to a mountain to pray.[95] Before choosing the Twelve, He goes up to a mountain and passes the night in communion with God.[96]

What a lesson for us! Instead of rushing immediately upon the work that awaits us, let us wait a while, recollect ourselves, purify our intention, and raise our minds to God. Especially when it is a question of forming and training His Apostles, our Lord spends time in prayer, as if to prove to us that we cannot succeed in changing the hearts of men without first imploring the help of God. And again, in order to ensure that His Apostles will gain a hearing from the world, our Lord prays likewise: "Not for them only do I pray, but for them also who through their word shall believe in me."[97]

---

[95] Matt. 14:23; Mark 6:46.
[96] Luke 6:12-13.
[97] John 17:20.

The Acts of the Apostles gives us a remarkable picture of St. Stephen. He was "full of grace and fortitude,"[98] we are told, and full of faith and the Holy Spirit. And because he was a man of God he had power over souls: "He did great wonders and signs among the people. . . . And they were not able to resist the wisdom and the spirit that spoke."[99]

When a soul possesses God, when a soul is in the state of grace, when it is also "possessed" by God, when it strives as often as possible to come into contact with God (the state of habitual recollection), then it can approach others. It may not be evident, even to the soul itself, that it is imparting divine powers to others; our Lord may sometimes permit that nothing is imparted to others. But in fact, through that soul, God will have found a way into certain other souls, and to others He will have revealed Himself more clearly. He who possesses God, and possesses Him in a heart that is free from encumbrances, cannot fail to have great influence upon his fellows.

---

[98] Acts 6:8.
[99] Acts 6:8, 10.

Part Two

*Approaching Others
About the Faith*

Chapter Four

Make Truth Visible to Those Around You

∞

The descent from Heaven is only the first stage in the conquest of souls. To save us, God willed to become incarnate. Following His example, and in a manner we shall examine later, every apostle must endeavor to do the same.

What does this mean?

It means that the apostle in his own person must, first, make the truth visible; and this will be the subject of the present chapter. Second, he must make the truth lovable by presenting it as attractively as he can. Third, he must make the truth admirable by becoming, as far as possible, a heroic example of Christian virtue. The latter two points will be explained in the following chapters.

To help us to achieve our destiny, God was not content merely to give us a conscience that would guide us according to the law of reason; He completed the natural law by a positive teaching: Revelation.

But of what use to most men are words, even divine words? Man always feels the need of seeing, touching, and feeling; and he does not allow himself to be easily won even by a divine word that is a word and nothing more. Throughout the whole of the Old Testament, we see how God endeavored to keep man in the path of duty by recalling to him the requirements of God's Word. But what does Jerusalem do? It pays no heed; and what is worse, it kills those who are sent to it; it stones the prophets.[100]

And so the Word becomes incarnate. The message, instead of remaining a mere message, becomes a living life among us. The Word becomes flesh.[101] And the gospel is more than a lesson — much more. It is an example.

A word by itself rarely has any motive power, is rarely dynamic. Let an officer show his men the written order received from his superior, that they are to "go over the top," to go and meet death. These are so many words on paper, and the men will not budge. But let the officer advance at the head of his company, and then the men will follow him.

⚶

Bear Christ's message in your person

You will not persuade men by talking to them, but you will if you let them see. When the philosopher lays down as a moral axiom: "So act that your manner of action may become a universal rule," the majority of men are not convinced. Universal rule? Who cares for that? The great advantage of the religion of Jesus our Savior is that it is not merely a form of belief to be accepted; it shows this formula alive in a being of flesh and blood. You may follow Aristotle[102] without knowing anything about Aristotle; you may follow Plato[103] or Kant[104]

---

[100]Matt. 23:37; Luke 13:34.

[101]John 1:14.

[102]Aristotle (384-322 B.C.), Greek philosopher.

[103]Plato (427-347 B.C.), Greek philosopher.

[104]Immanuel Kant (1724-1804), German philosopher.

without knowing anything about Plato or Kant. It is not a matter of their person; it is a matter of their teaching. The gospel is not merely a manifestation of the teaching of Christ; it is the manifestation of His Person.

To believe does not mean only adherence to a dead text, it means submission to a living Person. So St. John wrote in his first letter: "That which was from the beginning, which we have heard, which we have seen with our eyes, which we have looked upon and our hands have handled, of the Word of life . . . that which we have seen and have heard, we declare unto you."[105] "The life," he said, "was manifested."[106] And in the prologue of his Gospel, having written: "The Word was made flesh," he added: "We have seen His glory."[107]

Abstract language will move no one; embody it in a well-devised image and it will live. An abstract formula leaves men cold; give it a body and it will begin to act on them.

This is especially true of a rule of life. An ethical formula counts for little; example is everything. If Christ had called us to the practice of poverty solely by His teaching in the Sermon on the Mount — "Blessed are the poor"[108] — then few men would have sought blessedness in poverty. Christ lived a poor man: He was born poor; He died poor. It was more by His example than by His word that He drew Francis of Assisi[109] and

---

[105] 1 John 1:1, 3.
[106] 1 John 1:2.
[107] Cf. John 1:14.
[108] Matt. 5:3.
[109] St. Francis of Assisi (c. 1182-1226), founder of the Franciscan Order.

Charles de Foucauld[110] — and a legion of others more or less like them — to follow Him.

To talk is a good thing, but to act is much better. The Gospels show us what Jesus did and taught;[111] He did and taught, but notice: He began by doing. His whole life is summed up in the words: He did all things well.[112] Even His enemies have no fault to find with Him. "I find no cause in Him," said Pilate.[113] Nothing in Him is worthy of blame. All is perfection.

In the rites that He instituted, our Lord connected the granting of grace with a visible thing: the sacraments. It is always the same principle of incarnation. And if the Church, following the example of our Lord, recommends prayer in silence and solitude, she also preaches external devotion, the use of images, and the visible manifestations of the Liturgy.

The apostle, then, will strive to acquire the maximum of human and supernatural qualities. Human qualities are by no means the most important, admittedly. But they have — some of them at least — a power of attraction which certain of the virtues do not possess.

∞

Be open and amiable

The apostle must be as human as possible. Our Lord was a man in the fullest and most magnificent sense of the word.

---

[110]Charles de Foucauld (1858-1916), French explorer called the "Hermit of the Sahara."

[111]Acts 1:1.

[112]Cf. Mark 7:37.

[113]Luke 23:4.

Responsive to all the beauties of nature, He loved the wayside flower and the golden moss, the vine and the fig tree, the bright light of the heavens and the majesty of the Temple. Responsive to all His brethren, He was with them in their sorrows and their joys: He shed tears over Lazarus[114] and over Jerusalem;[115] He raised the son of the widow of Nain[116] and the little daughter of the officer Jairus;[117] and He joined amicably in the festivities of Cana and of Simon the Pharisee. He was not pontifical or sententious; He always showed Himself to be cordial, simple, and approachable.

His chief quality was His good nature — "a smiling self-abandonment." He knew all things, but He overwhelmed none with His learning. At the age of twelve He talked easily with the doctors of Israel; He amazed them,[118] but He gave no offense. His disciples, the multitude, and even His judges had to admit that in matters of divine knowledge He was an adept without equal.

This is self-evident, but He did not strive to make it evident. And side by side with that simplicity that is so attractive, there is a majesty so gentle, an air of greatness so modest, and a nobility of manner so spontaneous.

"A great gentleman," one of the Church Fathers called Him later; but there is nothing about Him of the "tower of ivory" — the portcullis is always open, and anyone may always enter

[114]John 11:35.
[115]Luke 19:41.
[116]Cf. Luke 7:11-13.
[117]Mark 5:35-43.
[118]Luke 2:47.

freely. "Suffer them to come to me,"[119] He says of the children, and the little ones, who are always at their ease with the truly great, know Him by instinct. His arms are always open.

Like Christ, the apostle must be human in the widest possible sense: able to understand all, to love all, to appreciate all: He must have "feelers"; he must possess the gift of sympathy; and he must acquire the highest possible degree of competence. Yet withal he must be ever modest.

We have spoken of humility, and how necessary it is if we are to attract people. An air of superiority, a show of greatness, always offends. Let your merit appear, but do not make a show of it. True nobility of character is always humble; great men of learning, great artists, great politicians, and great soldiers, in general, are modest — if they are not, something is lacking in their greatness, in their attractiveness.

Open-heartedness, competence, good nature, nobility of character and demeanor — all these united with an easy and affable manner. Such are the qualities that, although natural, are nonetheless most valuable in an apostle, especially in the young.

∞

Reveal Christ through your God-given gifts

If it is important to present a humanity richly endowed with human gifts, it is above all necessary that through our humanity we should show forth Christ, and manifest the beauty of life as lived according to the gospel. Perrèyve used to pray: "Jesus, when they see me, may they recognize Thee."

---

[119]Matt. 19:14; Mark 10:14; Luke 18:16.

A young apprentice who had been working only for a short time in a factory was asked by a priest: "Do your fellow workers know the gospel?" "No, they do not know the gospel." "Do they know Jesus Christ?" "No, they do not know Jesus Christ." "Or the Pope?" "No." "Or the bishop?" "No." "Or their parish priest?" "No." "Then listen: you are going to have the honor of making all these things known to your fellow workers. When they see you, they must learn something about this Christianity of which they know nothing. It is for you to radiate the gospel. When they see you, let them discover Jesus Christ!"

This is the essential mission of the apostle: to be a living witness to the greatness and beauty of Christianity; especially in the present day, when so many people have only false ideas, prejudices, or total lack of understanding concerning religion.

We are "messengers of light," as Paul Claudel put it. He was writing to Jacques Rivière: "You have the leisure; you have the intelligence; you are the messenger of light for these unfortunate souls. What will you answer when they accuse you before God and ask: 'What have you done with these talents?' "

We do not all have the same leisure, the same intelligence, or the same degree of instruction, but all of us, according to the gifts we have received, are bound to make the truth known by letting it shine forth in us. "You who have the light," asks Claudel again, this time addressing all Christians, "what are you doing with it?"

∞

Be like leaven in the world
May we not all make our own the prayer of writer Katherine Mansfield: "Lord, make me like crystal so that Thy light

may shine through me"? Light penetrates everywhere and, in penetrating, is not soiled. It is the work of the apostle to penetrate all sorts of surroundings, bringing with him the truth and love of Jesus Christ; and he must be able to go anywhere with impunity. "I pray not," said our Lord, speaking of His disciples, "that Thou shouldst take them out of the world, but that Thou shouldst keep them from evil."[120] It is so easy to let oneself be influenced by one's surroundings, to be crushed by the mass instead of penetrating it like leaven.

The Russian philosopher Nicolas Berdyaev wrote: "The masses — that is, the quantitative majority — have throughout history oppressed and persecuted the qualitative minority; those individual minds that are turned toward the heights of the sublime. History has evolved in favor of the average man, the masses; it is for them that the state was created, the family, juridical institutions, the school, the whole code of manners and customs. . . . It is the average man, the man of the masses, that has always dominated history, always demanded that everything should be done for him, for his interests, and on his level."[121]

The great danger of "the world" — in the sense in which our Lord speaks of the world — is that it drags things down to the level of the average; it spreads the slow poison of mediocrity. It may not directly instigate sin, but it awakens a fascination with all that makes a person weak in the face of sin; it dethrones the ideal, scorns enthusiasm, and tends to reduce everything to the level of the commonplace. It glories in

[120]John 17:15.
[121]Nicolas Berdyaev, *Esprit et Liberté,* 16-17.

omissions; its danger lies less in what it demands than in what it obstructs.

The man who lets himself be influenced by such an atmosphere loses his capacity for generous effort; he will never be one of the elite. Nominally he may remain upon the list of the workers, but it will be risky for them to make use of him. Not strong enough to resist, not fully enough convinced to react against the fascination of error, he is acted upon by others instead of acting upon them. Instead of leading the flock, it is the flock that leads him. Communion with those less good has made him less good; he has become "so-so" — one of the crowd. Is he leaven for the masses? On the contrary, he is part of the mass that needs to be leavened.[122]

Our Lord did not come for the sake of those who are well, but for those who are in need.[123] The soul that is lost interests Him far more than the ninety-nine that are just; the venturesome lamb that has fallen into the pit, far more than the flock that has returned dutifully home; the coin that has rolled behind the furniture,[124] far more than the fortune in the cashbox. His interest is in the prodigals: Mary Magdalene, the woman taken in adultery, Zacchaeus the publican, Simon the Pharisee, Barabbas, and His companions on the cross.

The preferences of the apostle should be of the same kind. But what integrity this demands, what moral beauty, what sanctity! Some, perhaps, may be tempted to escape the corrosive or weakening effect of such surroundings by avoiding too

[122]Cf. Matt. 13:33; Luke 13:20-21.
[123]Matt. 9:12; Mark 2:17.
[124]Cf. Luke 15:4, 7, 8.

much contact with the masses, by seeking only the company of their friends, of those who think like them and to whom they feel more readily attracted. It is so much more pleasant to consort with those who are like you, and with whom you have ideals and interests in common.

Such a method is disastrous. If the leaven is to act upon the mass, it must be mingled with it. If it is separate from the mass, it forgets its proper task. It is a leading axiom in Catholic Action[125] not to remove good elements from the surroundings in which they exist, but rather to sanctify them so that they may serve to elevate and improve their fellows.

In order to act effectively upon one's surroundings, one must live in those surroundings; and, given the necessary virtue and power of action, the closer the contact, the greater the influence will be.

[125]Organized religious activity on the part of the laity.

Chapter Five

∞

Lead Others to Love Truth

∞

The gospel has its austere side. As the French mathematician and moralist Blaise Pascal said, if it were nothing but geometry, few would refuse to accept it. That there are three Persons in God is not the truth that worries most people. The gospel contains a moral code. It demands a manner of acting and a behavior in which nature sees nothing but restraints, and therefore nature fears it.

And this is especially true of the young. At an age when senses, desire, and curiosity are beginning to awaken, any prospect of restraint is repellent.

It is a mistake, especially when approaching young people, to present the religion of our Lord and Savior Jesus Christ from the purely negative side — what is forbidden, what must not be done. Christianity thus appears as a barrier-religion — a religion that makes for the attenuation of being and life — whereas the gospel is essentially and chiefly quite the opposite.

The doctrine of our Savior offers a magnificent vista of expansion. The Son of God did not come to earth to bind us hand and foot, to impose various police regulations, more or less of an unreasonable character. If He became man, it was in order to bring us something unique, something absolutely extraordinary.

Is it not literally true that it has been said of us: "You are gods,"[126] and that we are to become "sons of God"?[127] Let us give to these expressions their fullness of Christian meaning.

First and foremost, the baptized must learn to appreciate the incomparable privileges they have received by that sacrament which, in making them Christians, has brought the Blessed Trinity to dwell in their souls, and given them power to live the divine life, if only they will, and so long as they will. Let us lift up our heads and bear proudly the proud dignity of our Baptism.

How few of the baptized appreciate this sublimest of all revelations: that God dwells in the man who is in the state of grace? This is the campaign that is most urgently needed: to help each and every one to realize fully, perhaps for the first time, the divine dignity that Baptism confers by engrafting us upon Christ Himself, making us a living member of the Mystical Body of Christ, which is the Church, communicating to us the very life of the Blessed Trinity, making us partners in the royal priesthood of Christ and His Church, uniting us in a common kinship with all our baptized brethren by this spiritual solidarity, which is the Communion of Saints, consecrating us as living chalices, as living temples to the personal and social worship of the true God.

∾

Concentrate on the good, not on sin

Does not this discovery fill us with enthusiasm? Let us beware in our spiritual lives of concentrating exclusively upon

---

[126]Ps. 81:6 (RSV = Ps. 82:6).
[127]Rom. 8:14.

sin. Sin becomes an obsession: one sees it everywhere; its power and its fascination are exaggerated — you would almost think that the power of Satan is equal to that of God, the power of the antichrist equal to that of Christ. Why give sin this halo? Why make it loom so large that it blocks all else out of sight?

Sin exists, of course. It would be foolish to deny it. But it exists in its own place, and that is not the first place. The first thing I must do is not to avoid sin, but to live the divine life. First comes the splendor of the state of grace — not sin and wickedness, which fill us with horror. True spiritual hygiene consists not in being hypnotized by the world of evil, but in concentrating upon the good, upon the world of God, upon the vision of light.

"It is not by the repugnance of ugliness," wrote Péguy, "that we must teach beauty, but by the attractiveness of beauty itself." He is right. Are we, or are we not, sons of a King? Are we, or are we not, sons of God? Are we, or are we not, living tabernacles of the Blessed Trinity? Are we, or are we not, living prolongations of Christ? This is what counts. This is more important than anything else.

There can be no doubt that, in consequence of this baptismal glory, we must always, in all circumstances, behave as a baptized person should behave, as behooves a living tabernacle of the Blessed Trinity, a child of the Redemption, one who is truly consecrated. And if the fulfillment of this royal program, if the task of making our work, our gestures, our words, thoughts, and feelings worthy of a baptized person entails sacrificing some indulgence, some visit, a drink or a movie, then let us be glad to make the sacrifice. Is this restriction? Not at all. We grow richer through this sacrifice. To transform the shapeless block of marble into the radiant statue of his dreams, the sculptor strikes and chips the marble. Is this to spoil his marble? No, it is to give it a new beauty.

It is one of the most subtle temptations of the Evil One to persuade you that self-conquest means self-weakening, that to train oneself means to enfeeble one's energies.

The philosopher Joseph Renan once said, in his skeptical and apparently detached manner: "Truth is perhaps an unpleasant thing." Claudel, writing to Jacques Rivière, rightly stigmatized "the detestable words of this hideous Renan," and tells how they revolted him even before his conversion. "Already in my heart I knew that the only true reality is joy in God, and that the man who knows it not will never do the work of an artist, as he will never do the work of a saint."

Novelist André Gide does not even retain the "perhaps" of the statement of Renan. For him it is a dogma. Having for a long time resisted the sting of the flesh,[128] he succumbed in the end, and — as the weak are wont to do — he tried to give an explanation of his fall. To fall, he said, is to become enriched. We should taste every joy, strike every note of the keyboard, drink at every source. No distinction is to be made between forbidden joys and healthy joys: all is good; all is healthy. You can never have too wide an experience. All honor to the man who has experienced everything, even the worst.

As if it did no harm to mix poison with pure flour! Truly it must take a massive credulity to accept such a sophistry. Evil does not enrich. Sin has no beauty; it fascinates man, it is true;

[128]Cf. 2 Cor. 12:7.

but in itself it is not fascinating. Man is attracted by a mirage. The Devil is not amusing. He can amuse, which is something quite different. This is not to say that he has in himself a power of attraction, but he can amuse because there is in us a power of misunderstanding and illusion, because we remain content with appearances and do not go to the heart of reality.

Evil is nonbeing; evil is a void. It may wear a mask, but that is what it is essentially. And, therefore, instead of developing our powers, it attenuates them; instead of giving true joy, it yields boredom. And that is proved by the experience of those who have reached a certain limit in evil. That taste of ashes in the mouth, that rancor, that emptiness — that is the true taste of sin. Evil is an unpleasant thing.

Away, then, with the theories of Renan and Gide — they are specious. Evil is evil, not because it is forbidden but because it is nonbeing. Essentially it is a privation, and to gratify one's appetites with a privation is not to become enriched. You might as well say that dry bread is equivalent to a good dinner.

We must oppose that custom whereby virtue is dissociated from the idea of happiness, and joy always associated with sin. It is sin that brings unhappiness. Virtue, whatever sacrifices it may entail, is really and truly that which gives joy.

It was Ernest Psichari, the grandson of Renan, who said, when he was definitely on the way to conversion: "I knew where I was going. I was going toward the abode of peace; I was going to joy. I wept with love, happiness, and gratitude." Claudel wrote in a similar strain to Jacques Rivière: "Whatever you may think, you will never approach happiness without approaching its source, which is God and Christ."

There you have the truth: approaching true joy means drawing near to God; to draw near to God is to draw near to true happiness.

∞

Present Christianity in a favorable light

Following the example of Christ, therefore, we must not present Christian doctrine, especially to the young, under an exclusively negative form. But that is not all — we must strive always to present it under its most attractive aspect.

Let us watch our Lord. How does He proceed?

He is preaching His Sermon on the Mount. He wishes to give to the world His great lessons of detachment, purity, and charity, and He knows well that these may easily cause the timid to shrink, and even the willing to hesitate. Accordingly, He avoids making a series of demands. He gives a recipe for happiness. Do you wish be happy? Then act thus and thus.

He puts in the foreground, not His rights, but our happiness. A recipe for happiness must surely be greeted with smiles. That would be worthy buying; anyone would pay a price for that.

Even when our Lord is speaking directly of the Cross and of the duty of practicing needful self-denial, He is careful to add the motive that allures: "If any man would come after me."[129] The service of God is presented as a friendship before it appears as a renunciation. A renunciation is repugnant, but a friendship attracts. And history shows that this friendship has appeared so attractive that multitudes of souls have chosen to

---

[129] Matt. 16:24; Luke 9:23.

follow our Lord, even to the length of giving up all, even to the most perfect imitation, even to the "folly of the cross."[130]

Let us use the same method in our apostolate. This is not to say that we are to use deceit in order to hide what Christian doctrine demands of us, but we should begin by pointing out the rich potentialities of development that Christian doctrine contains. Nobody is such a fool as to think that diamonds can be bought for a few cents. And no one will think that the precious pearl can be found without paying a price.[131] The important thing is to show the value of the pearl, to present it in a favorable light. Arouse enthusiasm. Sacrifice will follow.

[130]Cf. 1 Cor. 1:18.
[131]Cf. Matt. 13:46.

Chapter Six

Make the Truth
Admirable

❧

To present Christian doctrine in all its positive richness — and even, where it demands sacrifices, to insist upon the fullness of life that such sacrifices develop — is already a method that will bear much fruit. But we must do more.

We have to make Christian teaching attractive by presenting it in action, by furnishing an example of Christian life that will be not only attractive, but, if possible, even heroic. We have to make the truth admirable.

Words may be effective, but actions have a hundred times their value in power of persuasion. And among actions, the most persuasive of all are those that are marked with the stamp of heroism. That is why St. John the Baptist won so many disciples. He was, as the Gospel says, "a burning and a shining light," and for that reason many were "willing to rejoice in his light."[132]

With our Lord it was the same. He attracted more by His example than by His words; and if He attracted men more than did St. John the Baptist, it was because the example that He gave to the world and the wonders that He worked far surpassed those of the precursor. "I have a greater testimony than that of John, for the works which the Father hath given me to

---

[132]John 5:35.

perfect, the works themselves which I do, give testimony of me, that the Father hath sent me."[133]

And the works that the Father gave Him to perfect were not only His miracles; there was also the astounding sanctity of His life: heroism in poverty and detachment; in His courage before the Pharisees and before His judges; in accepting suffering; and in His love for men.

Why is the example of Christ so alluring? Not merely because it is an example, but because it is an example of such extreme devotedness that it compels admiration, and in those who fully appreciate it, it engenders an immeasurable love.

To appreciate the poverty of our Lord, it is enough to look at the manger. Joseph and Mary were poor, but at least they had their home at Nazareth. Yet they had to leave their home, and Jesus was born in a stable. Surely He would be allowed to pass the early years of His infancy in the home of His parents. No. There was Herod, the persecution, and the massacre of the Innocents;[134] He had to flee into Egypt. Later, during His public life, He depended upon the chance hospitality accorded Him; He had not a stone on which to lay His head.[135]

And His courage in facing the Pharisees and His judges! When the sellers desecrated the Temple, He did not hesitate to take the scourge in hand against them.[136] He laid bare the malice of the faithless and hypocritical Pharisees, and when they raved about the empty observance of the law, He showed

---

[133]John 5:36.
[134]Matt. 2:16; 13.
[135]Cf. Matt. 8:20; Luke 9:58.
[136]John 2:14-15.

how vain is a worship that has no soul. Envy and hatred pursued Him in consequence. But of that He took no heed. Before His judges, He knew that if He stated the truth openly, it would cost Him His life. Not for a moment did He hesitate.

And with what calm tranquillity He accepted suffering! He knew what the salvation of the world would cost Him. He was offered because He willed it. He had to die by a cruel crucifixion: "For our sake He was crucified."[137] And the motive of His sacrifice was His love for fallen humanity, for a humanity shorn of all its divine perfections. He who loves gives up his life. "Greater love no man hath."[138] "He loved them unto the end."[139]

The more capable an apostle is of presenting a heroic embodiment of virtue, the better he will be as an apostle. Men surrender to whatever surpasses the ordinary. We need something far more than ordinary virtue. Average people as a rule achieve little; to attract the masses and carry them with you, you must stand above the common level. St. Ignatius[140] required of his companions that they should be "outstanding" in the service of God; he demanded something far more than a half-hearted service, more than "carpet-slipper" loyalty.

Every apostle must aim at being an outstanding apostle; he must strive to reproduce in himself the qualities of his Master:

[137]From the Nicene Creed.

[138]John 15:13.

[139]John 13:1.

[140]St. Ignatius Loyola (c. 1495-1556), founder of the Society of Jesus.

outstanding detachment, outstanding boldness, outstanding spirit of sacrifice, and outstanding charity.

∞

Be detached, bold, and charitable

It would be impossible, in these days, to exaggerate the importance of detachment from the comforts of life, if any influence is to be exerted upon one's fellowmen. Our age is an age of frenzied love of pleasure — the masses, the herd, wants only self-indulgence. They say: "Between the past war, during which we were too much restricted, and the conflagrations to come, during which we shall have perforce to be restricted again, let us open the sluices and let ourselves go: every pleasure, every satisfaction, the body, the flesh, nudism in theory and in practice, erotic publications flourishing, attacks on the marriage laws, the quest for artificial and sophisticated pleasures, casinos, gaming dens, cinemas, gambling, and jobbery — anything, as long as you have money to buy it."

We need a Francis of Assisi. Today more than ever, the world needs to learn contempt for all that is transitory, for the false glitter of worldly joys, and to follow only one Master: Christ.

The task before the apostle is to recreate the code of Christianity in a pagan world, and that is a task that calls for heroes. To give life to the inert, to bury the corpse, to arouse enthusiasm, to persuade the masses to receive the leaven and react to it — all this needs something more than lukewarm Christians.

"I realize the immense work that we have to do in ourselves before we can make any impression. The masses are gross, bestial, although there are some fine characters. Above all, there is much of the herd instinct, and the quest for pleasure. You need to be strong to make any impression there, and the ordinary good fellow is not the man to succeed. People will have nothing to do with that type. I have often noticed how much unbelievers demand of believers before they will admire or follow them. They will only submit to the influence of the strong. Anything in the nature of affectation, softness, or readiness to compromise is already condemned beforehand."[141]

There is no need to be afraid of asking too much. What attracts the young especially is the hard task, the difficult exploit. If you want volunteers for easy work, they are not enthusiastic. When faced with the choice of a religious order, souls that have a vocation seem by instinct to adopt those orders that are more fervent and more exacting. Similarly, souls will only enroll themselves in the service of a leader or an organization if they see that there are sacrifices to make and hard work to do.

Moreover, today we need charity, a great-hearted charity. One cannot love too much. Francis of Assisi and Charles de Foucauld impressed the world by their poverty, but still more by their charity.

It is not so easy to love. We are speaking here of Christian love — that is, supernatural love. The world can love in a human way, but we have to love in a divine way — that is, we must see in others, however little they may attract our human love, the presence of the Lord and the seal of Christ. We must learn to recognize what the eyes of the body cannot see and

[141]Jacques Maritain, *Jean Baron*, 166, 173, 177.

what only faith can reveal. We do not sufficiently understand the Communion of Saints. In certain quarters today, admitting that you love something is enough to make you fall into disgrace. It is the unpardonable sin.

Admittedly, there are different ways of loving, and we are not advocating that form of humanitarianism which has no consistency or laws, and which has nothing in common with the charity of Christ.

Before talking of love as between class and class, and nation and nation, should we not ask ourselves what sort of love we bear toward our fellow workers, or our brethren in the social circle in which we live our daily lives?

Part Three

Giving of Yourself

Chapter Seven

∞

Be Courageous
in Following Christ

∞

To win souls for Christ, the apostle must first stoop to souls as the Son of God did. He must adapt himself to them, put himself on their level and within their reach. And he must do this not as one who comes from the same region as they, but as one who comes from the serene heights of prayer, from Heaven, from God. Next, he must transform his words into example — and, if possible, into so transcending an example as to attract the souls of others. This is a great deal to do. But it is not yet enough.

He who desires to exercise his power of redeeming to the utmost limit, as Christ did, must not shrink from that which awaits all saviors: the Cross. Souls are won by words, and they are won by example, but above all, they are won by sacrifice. "When I am weak," wrote St. Paul, "then I am powerful."[142] In this conflict, it is those who fall who are victorious; the salvation of the world belongs to the crucified.

∞

Embrace sacrifice

Suffering means, in the first place, to embrace the sacrifice that is necessary in order to destroy anything in oneself that

[142] 2 Cor. 12:10.

may obstruct the work of redemption. It is a negative task, but an essential and indispensable one. It costs a lot to become a Christian, a true Christian. To be perfect as our heavenly Father is perfect is no small thing.[143] And I may not aspire to anything less. I must not rest until "Christ is formed in me,"[144] as St. Paul and the gospel require. My vocation as a Christian means that I must become "another Christ," a living continuation of Jesus our Savior; to that I am called by my Baptism. But to this transformation into Jesus Christ, to this "transubstantiation," as one might call it, my lower nature offers a thousand obstacles.

Paul said: "I live now, not I, but Christ liveth in me."[145] But I am far from being able to say the same; the "I" is very strong in me, it lives vigorously and asks only to live an even fuller life. The slightest sacrifice costs me a lot — to do somebody a favor, to give up some food that I like, to give up a dance, to resist excessive curiosity in looking at a passerby, to correct untidy habits, or to devote myself diligently to my work — such things for me are an affair of state.

At the Consecration in the Mass, the bread is inert matter, and when the irresistible words — "This is my Body" — are pronounced, there is nothing left of the bread; it is all instantaneously changed into Jesus Christ.

But my nature is not inert; it is a living reality. And it cannot be changed in an instant, because every particle of "me" offers resistance. It feels that it is wrong to offer resistance,

[143]Cf. Matt. 5:48.
[144]Gal. 4:19.
[145]Gal. 2:20.

that it ought to offer itself to so desirable a transformation, but courage is lacking. Moreover, the atmosphere that surrounds us is not propitious to renunciation. Nothing invites us to a life of detachment; and if events demand sacrifice, especially for the sake of Christ, the majority turn a deaf ear, and only accept it with grumblings and complaints at the privations they are forced to undergo.

Yet in worldly affairs people do not mind making sacrifices. A woman can display immense courage and energy to save her husband from a Soviet camp; and yet it would seem that we are incapable of making the smallest renunciation for the sake of Christ!

Think of the young fellow who lost his eyes during the war, but made up his mind that it would make no difference to him. He continued to ride a bicycle and a horse; he took up the study of law, became a barrister, studied his briefs, and pleaded in court; he took up politics, studied the newspapers, devoted himself to the questions of the day, and became a member of the Chamber of Deputies — and when interviewed was able to say: "If I have lost ninety percent of my capacity for happiness, my capacity for work has remained the same." If he could make that generous effort merely to retain his place among men, can we not show a little energy on behalf of Christ?

Beethoven, the great musician who was later to be afflicted with deafness, said: "Sacrifice all the follies of life to your art." In 1796, he wrote in his diary: "In spite of my bodily weakness, my genius will triumph. I am twenty-five years old. This very year, the whole man must reveal himself."

And our eighteen, twenty, twenty-five years? What are we going to do with them for Christ?

Chapter Eight

Abandon All
to Win the World
to Christ

∞

Sacrifice is necessary as a preliminary condition of the apostolate: you cannot be a savior unless you are "another Christ," and you cannot be "another Christ" unless you are, to some extent, at any rate, crucified as Christ was. But we must go further and say: sacrifice is important as being the principal means of winning souls — and first, because of its value as an example.

Of those who do not accept the gospel, few deny that the gospel possesses the one true way of salvation. But what many of them seek — and seek in vain, unfortunately — are preachers of the gospel who begin by living what they demand of others.

Garric put the matter very well when he wrote: "The world today awaits a St. Francis of Assisi as an apostle of peace. But St. Francis had first renounced his mantle and his robe. Who among us has stripped himself?"

It is not enough in the present day to "talk" — if indeed it ever was enough. We must show the world how the gospel is lived. Speakers are not lacking; indeed there is a glut of them. It is not people who are ready to mount the platform that we need, so much as people who are ready to mount the Cross.

So many people are so easily satisfied! Their hearts are not open to great things. An average personality, average happiness, average ideals are enough for them. They are content to be one of the herd.

∞

Don't settle for the world's ideals

What our Lord demands of His Apostles is to beware of being ordinary, to be a contrast to the masses — not through vanity but for the sake of their apostolate — and to love the Cross in the midst of a world that denied the Cross. "Follow me," He says, "and I will make you fishers of men."[146]

"Follow me. Leave the ordinary, the commonplace. Leave comfort and egoism. Be willing to suffer. Be willing to be unlike others, to cut yourself off from everything that is not me — only on this condition can the work of the apostle be done. Follow me: on this condition, and on this condition alone, 'I will make you fishers of men.' " And to St. Peter in particular our Lord said: "Henceforth thou shalt catch men"[147] — that is, when he had accepted the necessary detachment from all things of earth.

And what was the response of the Apostles? They knew what had been their Master's lot. They would have to brave fatigue, as Jesus was "wearied with His journey"; thirst, as Jesus suffered at Jacob's well;[148] and hunger, as "He was hungry."[149] If this was the lot of their Master, could they hope for greater comfort?

[146]Cf. Matt. 4:19; Mark 1:17.
[147]Luke 5:10.
[148]John 4:6-7.
[149]Matt. 4:2.

And in this sense they understood their mission. They were fond of their nets, but they gave up their nets. They were fond of their own country, but they left their own country. They were like the African who, being asked by a European what his country was, answered: "My country is the whole earth."

And it requires perhaps as much self-denial to open one's heart to embrace all, as to shut one's heart in privation; as much self-denial to be willing to conquer the earth when one is a stay-at-home, as to give up some little thing to which one is attached.

∽

Be prepared for resistance

The sacrifices of the body are not the most painful. The most painful are the sacrifices of the soul: renunciation of self-love, readiness to submit to unjust or foolish judgments, suspicions, ridicule, and the open or covert opposition of those whom one is trying to arouse to enthusiasm. "I am not come to bring peace but the sword," said Jesus.[150] And that is what He meant.

In the same sense, He said: "Behold, I send you as sheep in the midst of wolves,"[151] and "You shall be hated for my name's sake."[152] "Christ is not come to be ministered unto but to minister, and to give his life [as] a redemption for many."[153] "Unless

---

[150]Cf. Matt. 10:34.
[151]Matt. 10:16.
[152]Matt. 10:22, 24:9; Mark 13:13; Luke 21:17.
[153]Matt. 20:28; Mark 10:45.

the grain of wheat falling into the ground dies, it remaineth alone. But if it dies, it bringeth forth much fruit."[154]

It is childish to think that you can work for the advancement of the kingdom of God without encountering vigorous resistance. The brute in man always kicks against the message of Christ. Before the invitation of the Spirit, the "sensual man,"[155] as St. Paul calls him, shies and protests.

In the early days of Christianity, when the faithful wanted to spread the reign of detachment, chastity, and charity, worldly men quickly sent for tigers and panthers to tear them to pieces in the amphitheaters, or for a company of soldiers to cut off their heads. St. Paul tells us of the torments he had to undergo because he had dared to preach the gospel of Christ.[156] And there is not a single corner of the earth where the kingdom of our Savior has been founded without meeting resistance.

These texts and these facts are pregnant with meaning. To think that you can work for the salvation of the world without, directly or indirectly, partaking in the sacrifice of the Savior of the world, is imagination pure and simple. Our Lord was quite frank with His Apostles when He sent them forth on their mission: "Can you drink of the chalice which I shall drink?" Only when they had answered that they could did He confide to them the task of saving their brethren.[157]

Our Lord asks us, too: "Can you drink of the chalice? Can you bear your part in your Master's sufferings?" What answer

---

[154]Cf. John 12:24-25.
[155]1 Cor. 2:14.
[156]2 Cor. 11:23-28.
[157]Matt. 20:22-23.

are we going to give? Shall we desert? Or shall we, like the Apostles, answer generously: "Yes, Lord, we can."

∞

Accept your missionary role

Sacrifice wins by force of example, and we have seen that Christ demanded it of those whom He made His first Apostles. But there is a deeper reason that goes down to the roots of dogma.

After Original Sin, by which the human race lost its divine life, Christ came to buy it back for us, but not as a benefactor who pays for us from without: He made us one with Him. He would be the one possessor of the divine life, but with Him we would be united, as the members are united to the Head.

Now, what method did Christ choose in order to ensure the salvation of the world? He taught men by His example and by His words, and that is why we, too, must exercise the apostolate by a faithful life and by courageous words. He prayed for souls, and that is why we must apostolize our brethren by praying for them. But the chief saving instrument is the Cross; and that is why, if we understand our mission as saviors of souls with Christ the Savior, we must accept the Cross and even seek it.

Christ might have saved the world without us. But He did not choose to do so. He deigned to will that we should "make up what is wanting of the sufferings of Christ."[158] Can anything be lacking in a sacrifice that is of infinite value? In itself, no. But in fact, our Lord leaves us our part of the work to

[158]Cf. Col. 1:24.

accomplish. The reason He has made us one with Him is in order that we may be able to pay our share. It is the *whole* Christ who must save the world; since I am a living member of the whole Christ, I have a mission, a function to fulfill.

That is the essential word: mission. Everyone who is baptized, if he understands the part he has to play, is a missionary. He may not be called upon to go to foreign lands; his apostolate may be destined only to affect his near neighbors. But he must understand that wherever he may happen to be, he has a function to perform there: he not only has to save himself, but he also has to sanctify and save his brethren. And for that he needs to be an example, certainly, like his Master; he needs words, too, and certainly prayer. But above all, he needs the Cross, sacrifice.

It remains to see now what this sacrifice may be.

Chapter Nine

∞

Offer Up Small Sacrifices for Others

∞

Among the various sacrifices that the apostle is called upon to make for the sanctification and salvation of his brethren is the sacrifice of *time*.

There is great merit in sacrificing the time that is destined for pleasure, rest, and leisure — especially in an age when pleasure is of all things the most tempting. But let this be clearly understood: it is not a question of stealing hours or minutes from the duties of one's state. Before you think of busying yourself with your neighbor, even if it is to procure him the greatest benefit in the world (except for the case of his extreme need), you must give to God what He expects of you yourself.

Now, those who seek to devote themselves to apostolic labors find that they are called upon to take part in a multitude of good works. And it sometimes happens that, to fulfill all their engagements, they have to dissipate their energies to the detriment of their apostolate, or else to neglect some important duty of their lives. The great need is for unity and centralization. With so many different forms of activity being inaugurated every day, it is difficult to see to which of them one should devote one's energies.

These various forms of apostolate are doubtless necessary in order to satisfy every taste. But let each man undertake only what he can frankly reconcile with his own state of life. Many would be well advised to undertake less, and the creators of new enterprises might well be asked whether there is not already in existence something of the same kind, or something very like it. If there is, then let them leave it at that. It is possible to have too much of a good thing.

∞

Be willing to sacrifice your reputation

It is difficult to sacrifice one's time, but it is still more difficult to sacrifice one's reputation. A young man who devotes himself to the apostolate soon finds himself labeled; he finds himself regarded as a weakling or a hypocrite; he is called a "choirboy," or some other amiably scornful name. And there is nothing that young men hate more than to be laughed at. Opposition or hatred they do not mind. But there are few who have the courage to face sarcasm.

Let them remember the words of our Lord to His Apostles: "You will be hated for my name's sake."[159] It is all foreseen, and the apostle should know it; you cannot fight for Jesus Christ without risking sarcasm for the sake of Jesus Christ. Do not be afraid of it; let it pass.

Have we not many examples of men striving for a purely human ideal, who show the utmost contempt for what others may think of them? On his return from Rome, Cardinal Liénart, addressing an audience of young men, quoted what the Holy Father had said to him about devotion to Soviet doctrine in Russia: "These people have an ideal. They are

[159]Cf. Matt. 10:22; Mark 13:13.

captivated by it. When necessary, they are capable of suffering for it and even of risking their lives in defense of it. That is strength." The Pope added: "And we, have we not, a higher ideal? If we Catholics could all be captivated by that ideal to the extent of suffering something, and if necessary even risking our lives to realize it, then the victory would be ours."

We may not be called upon to risk our lives; it is simply a matter of facing a sneer. Is the cause of Christ not worth that? At the beginning of every bold enterprise, there have been men who scorned the sneers of scoffers. Were there not plenty of people to laugh at Christopher Columbus and his plans, and, more recently, at those who dreamed of ascending to the stratosphere by using the force of the tides? And when the question of the subway in Paris was first raised, crowds of jokers declared it impossible, and when the compressed air brake was discovered, there was no lack of joyful prophets to declare that it was impossible to stop railway engines with wind.

∞

Be willing to sacrifice little things

Besides the sacrifice of time and the sacrifice of reputation, there is also simply the sacrifice which is necessary in order to assure the triumph of the cause that we are defending. There is, for example, the sacrifice of light or amusing books in favor of a deeper study, which will give us a greater competence in our work, and greater powers of conquest.

Can I restrain myself? I have great ambitions, I aspire to great and generous sacrifices, I want to suffer for my Master, to carry the Cross with Him . . . and I cannot even do this little thing. I am like the character described by Georges Duhamel in one of his novels: "He would give his life, but not this slice of mutton."

That is just it. God will probably not ask my life of me; what He would like me to give is just these little things — my "slice of mutton," my ten dollars that go up in smoke — but I have not the courage to do it. And I think I am the stuff that apostles are made of!

However, we must be patient, we must train ourselves; we must make a beginning. "The threshold of the door," said a Danish proverb, "is the highest mountain in the world." It is true. It is not giving up smoking that is hard; it is the beginning of giving up smoking. Likewise, it is not difficult to pray; it is difficult to begin to pray. Beginnings are always difficult.

Admittedly, when the first step has been taken, there still remains much to be done. Virtue necessarily presupposes not only the energy to undertake, but also the generosity to persevere and the courage to accomplish. But it is a great deal to have begun. Indeed, well begun is half done — perhaps even three-quarters.

At a meeting of young men, a student thus addressed his companions: "Where are these apostles coming from, these famous apostles who are going to change everything? . . . As soon as we have people who are real Christians and real men, then we shall have apostles.

"What sort of men do we want? Men capable of heroism even to the extent of shedding their blood? Yes, but first of all, men who have courage enough to get out of bed in the morning when the bell rings. Do we want men capable of putting into practice the ancient discipline of asceticism? Yes, but first of all, men who have enough faith in the Redemption and the

Eucharist to go to Mass sometimes during the week, and to go to Communion more often than once a month, more often than every Sunday. Do we want men capable of becoming missionaries of the gospel to the people? Yes, but first of all, men who think of other things than dancing, riding, spending their evenings playing bridge, or wasting endless hours in cafes."

Each can examine and see what he ought to deny himself. The essential problem for each is this: Do I want to be an apostle — yes or no? If you do, then go ahead and make the necessary sacrifices.

If you want to be one of those who win souls for Jesus Christ, you must renounce an easy and comfortable existence. It is not from these that the salvation of the world will come.

Happy are those who have been educated to sacrifice by a disciplined upbringing. Those who have not received such an education must educate themselves in this way. They must, in the words of Claudel, "make acquaintance with iron and steel; they must learn the healthy athletic joys of self-conquest." And so that this program may have an apostolic bearing, keep in mind the words of Jacques d'Arnoux: "Sacrifices are the jewels that God gives you in order to save your brethren. In return, you give him only gravel; you are a coiner. To give these diamonds their infinite value, resignation is not sufficient. Come, take advantage of the days of prosperity to give alms to the poor and sorrowful. Waste nothing; give everything. Be munificent."

We are told in the book of Exodus that when Moses was commanded by God to build the tabernacle, the Israelites brought and laid before the feet of the prophet gold and silver,

bronze, purple dyes, linen, flocks, woods of all kinds, oil, per-
fumes, and various sorts of stones. Of all these the Lord would
make a tabernacle, He said, and He would dwell in the midst
of them.[160]

If the temple of Christianity is to be built, every apostle
must make his plentiful contribution of generous sacrifice.
The offerings may be varied — it is desirable that they should.
Upon their number and their quality depends the building of
the kingdom of God.

[160]Exod. 25:3-8.

Part Four

Forgetting Self
to Serve Others

Chapter Ten

∞

Work for
God's Glory

∞

There is a thing more terrible than dying, and that is being buried; I mean being buried alive.

Taking part in the work of redemption means following the Master even to that length. "He came down from Heaven, became incarnate, died, and was buried."

But, you will say, Jesus was not buried alive when He was taken down from the Cross. Agreed, and it is not of this burial that we wish to speak, although the symbolic value of this is not to be neglected. We mean here another burial by which Jesus was buried alive: His burial as the Word, together with the Father and the Holy Spirit, in the souls of men by sanctifying grace — or His burial as the Word Incarnate in our tabernacles.

Is it not characteristic of the divine activity that the more completely the immediate agent is hidden, the more effectively that power is displayed? Would we ever have thought of this as the most effective means by which God could act upon men: that He would imprison Himself for twenty-four hours out of every twenty-four, in the innumerable tombs of our tabernacles, unknown and forgotten; that He should shut Himself up in the heart of man, and there, unknown and unfelt, move man's will, enlighten his mind, and give a divine orientation to his activity?

How discreet is this buried God within us! It would seem that He fears to frighten us by too manifest a presence — that He fears to impose Himself upon our wills in such a way as to diminish the freedom of our consent. So delicate and so discreet is His action that, afterward, when we try to point to the exact moment in which that divine action began, we frequently find it impossible to do so. It is the triumph of the imperceptible.

The lesson of all this is clear enough: in order to act upon our souls, God buries Himself.

The great secret of a fruitful apostolate is to be buried. The most successful apostles are not those who make the greatest show, and the best successes are not those that are most apparent. The most solid articles in a journal are not always those that are signed by great names — a page may be excellent, and yet its author may be unknown.

Was not the war won more by "unknown soldiers" than by men whose names history will cherish? In the history of the salvation of souls, much might be written concerning the success of failures and the vicissitudes of retarded successes. It would make interesting and surprising reading.

Look at Christ's apparent failures! Did the young man who came to Him full of ardor and zeal, seeking a life of perfection, follow His advice? No, he went away sorrowful, and the Gospel loses all trace of him.[161] When Christ foretold the Eucharist to the Jews, some said: "This saying is hard, and who can hear it?"[162] And consider the ingratitude of the lepers who

[161]Matt. 19:21-22.
[162]John 6:61 (RSV = John 6:60).

were cleansed,[163] and the paralytics who were cured,[164] and the narrow outlook even of those who were very close to Christ!

∞

Do not seek immediate results

But have patience. A building cannot rise until great numbers of stones have been buried in the earth to give it a foundation. Think of Lisieux, and the hill upon which the basilica stands. Think of the rubble that had to be buried before even the smallest wall could rise above the soil. Plans had been made. But hard facts caused the plans to be changed: the soil was unstable; it was slipping. Tons of concrete had to be poured in; otherwise nothing would have held.

Souls, too, are so unstable. Who can tell the generosity that has to be poured into their foundations before they decide to hold fast? In the days when it took hundreds of years to build a cathedral, do you think that the architect of the early beginnings ever saw the completion of his plan? The man who lays the foundation stone is not always the man who lays the top stone of the pinnacle. And it is better so. If every sower, whether sowers of cathedrals or sowers of souls, saw the completion of his work, he might perhaps be too proud. Christ saves them from this danger.

Sometimes it is even worse. Solid foundations may be laid, and yet on those foundations nothing will be built, nothing will be raised above the soil. But Christ does not need those who raise; He needs those who hide themselves. From generous

[163]Luke 17:17-18.
[164]Cf. Matt. 9:6-7.

zeal that has been buried in one corner of a field, Christ can raise up wonders of grace in the opposite corner.

In the invisible world, what is apparently of no use at all is often that which serves best. A failure well accepted by an apostle who has displayed all his energy to succeed is more salutary than many a triumph. The triumph might have occasioned a little pride. Humility is pure gold; and with that money, the debt of many can be paid.

And so, apostle, cast your seed tirelessly. Be not solicitous about what may become of it. "Sow the seed," said a holy soul, Marie-Antoinette de Geuser, "without looking to see where it falls." Zeal with detachment: that is what is needed — no ostentation, no outward show.

Go even further, and thank God in advance for the apostolic results of your failures. That will be a good act of faith. Perhaps what happened to Christ will happen also to you. When He spoke to that young man, he would not understand Him, but how many young men in the course of ages will recall Christ's words to him! It seemed a failure, but what a success withal! And you know how they murmured and went away when Christ spoke to them of the Eucharist. But see how many since then have come to Him, hungry for the living Bread.[165] It was a setback, but what a triumph, too!

The same will happen to you. You will speak, and at moments you will not be heard. But later one of your hearers whose heart had been closed will open it. You will act, and at the moment, your zeal will be stillborn. But someday, when you do not know it, some soul will be touched and will receive

[165]John 6:51.

life through you. Be thankful in anticipation for this delayed and obscure success.

My Lord, I will use Your precious lessons in the work of my youthful apostolate. Saviors come forth from the tomb. Teach me to bury myself.

Chapter Eleven

Work for the
Long Term

∞

Let us recall what has been said before: it is not his own cause that the apostle promotes and defends, but God's. His zeal must never puff him up. St. John the Baptist said: "He must increase, and I must decrease."[166] St. Paul goes further. He must not only decrease; he must disappear altogether. "I live, now not I; but Christ it is that liveth in me."[167] Hence the important consequence: we must avoid, as we would the plague, any jealousy toward those who are working with us and who have better success than we.

One day the Apostles were going with Jesus to Capernaum, and they were a little ahead of Him, deep in some discussion. On their arrival at the village, Jesus, who had noticed their animated conversation, asked them: "What did you speak of on the way?" The poor Apostles held their peace, being covered with shame, "for on the way, they had disputed among themselves which of them should be the greatest."[168]

The ABC of the hidden apostolate involves submitting with a good grace to being the least — not sounding one's own trumpet, not minding being an apparently insignificant cog in

[166]John 3:30.
[167]Gal. 2:20.
[168]Cf. Mark 9:32-33 (RSV = Mark 9:33-34).

the machinery, and leaving the best, or at any rate, the most important part, to others. There are many who never succeed in deciphering these elementary letters, and they remain beginners forever.

It is a curious thing to see how many great works have no known author. What a number of cathedrals there are whose architect is unknown! How many famous paintings, sculptures, writings, and inventions there are of which we shall never know who was the genius who brought them out of the limbo of nothingness!

Take, for example, the brazen disk under the Arch of Triumph, from which issues the flame that celebrates the memory of the unknown soldier. Is there anybody who has not seen it? But ask the passersby if they know the name of the man who first thought of the idea, who first planned it, or the name of the metal worker who executed it.[169] Nobody knows. It is not only the unknown soldier who lies buried under the Arch of Triumph, together with him are buried those who have striven to sing his praises.

And there are countries that have been discovered and that do not bear the name of the first man to land upon them. Christopher Columbus was the first to reach the mainland of the New World; but it was not he, but Amerigo Vespucci, a Florentine who set out upon a second expedition, who unwittingly gave his name to the newly discovered continent. The Queen of Spain had promised a great sum to the first seaman

---

[169] It was the architect Henry Favier, a modest man who has produced many works of art that do not bear his name, who first suggested the plan that was subsequently adopted.

under the command of Columbus to sight the coast they sought. The leader of the expedition had himself promised the fortunate man a silken doublet. They were vain offers — not a name has come down to posterity. We do not know who was the first to see America.

And if this is the case with human affairs and enterprises, it is much more so with the affairs and enterprises of God. Discoveries, creations, and institutions remain. The discoverers, the creators, and the institutors are often unknown, or else they have soon fallen into oblivion. Such is the triumph of hidden zeal.

∽

Do not be discouraged by failure

The second important thing for the apostle to remember is that he must not allow himself to be disappointed if the work upon which he has set his heart ends in failure. The generous acceptance of failure in advance does much to promote the cause of God. God wants virtue rather than triumphs. And who knows whether an apparent failure may prove to be a real triumph, although it may remain hidden? God, who lives in an eternal present, may, in a far-off place at some remote time, grant graces that would otherwise have been refused.

Put into the foundations of your work all the effort you can — intelligent and detached effort. Never give up until you have tried everything. But when you have done that, acknowledge that you have done nothing, and that grace alone can bring the work to fruition.

Have boundless trust in God. Many generous efforts come to nothing because there has been too much self-confidence.

Count only on God. Live by faith. Believe in the omnipotence and infinite subtlety of grace.

What Péguy said is quite true: "Grace is insidious; grace is cunning and unexpected. When grace does not come directly, it comes indirectly. When it does not come from the right, it is coming from the left. When it does not come straight, it is because it is coming on a curve; and when it does not come on a curve, it is because it is coming in bits. When it wants somebody, it has him. It does not take the same roads as we do; it makes its own. It does not even take its own, for it never takes the same road twice. When it does not come from above, it is because it is coming from below; and when it does not come from the center, it is because it is coming from the circumference. And the water of this spring, when it does not come forth as from a gushing fountain, may trickle like the water that oozes under the dikes of the Loire."

If grace is the most important character in the drama of the sanctification and salvation of souls, it follows that the apostle is only a minor actor; necessary indeed because God has willed it so, but one whose place is more behind the scenes than on the stage. He is there to change the general appearance of things, to allow God to vary His technique, and to bring about the victorious ending in a different way.

Remember that although grace is powerful, it is slow in its action. God could work quickly if He willed. He chooses not to. He has the whole of eternity at His disposal. When the farmer has sown his seed in the furrow, he does not come out the next morning to see whether it has grown yet. No, he knows that the seed takes time to germinate. It may take weeks, even months.

Apostles, especially young apostles, are always in a hurry: they want to see the harvest the day after the seed has been sown. You do not convert a soul or a group of souls quickly. "You cannot bear them now," said our Lord one day to His disciples.[170] "You cannot now understand what I am preaching to you, but you will later. Have patience."

∞

Be mindful of the future

Precisely because you are willing not to hurry matters, you will have confidence in the future. One of the most necessary qualities for an apostle is "a sense of the future" — that is, to be able not only to wait patiently, but also to foresee the method that will be necessary in order to reach souls more effectively.

Alain Chartier, a professor of philosophy, in taking leave of his pupils made the following commentary upon the parable of the wise and foolish virgins:[171] "They fell asleep while awaiting the bridegroom, and they are condemned to follow him from afar carrying their empty lamps. What a beautiful symbol! How many there are that spend their whole lives following after an event, always too late for it because they have fallen asleep waiting for it. Mark well, the event will come like a thief, and you must await it with eyes open and with lamps burning." He added: "It is not enough to live on the dreams of the day before yesterday; we must have a thought also for tomorrow."

[170]John 16:12.
[171]Matt. 25:1-13.

Abbé de Tourville gave the same advice in more vigorous terms: "Let us live in the present like men who have come from the future. . . . One of our trials is that we see the good more clearly than others [do]. You will say that the good is clear in itself, and that everybody ought to see it. I agree, but remember that Christopher Columbus did not succeed in making people understand his plan. And yet there was no malice in them. In other matters, besides the discovery of America, we find the same sort of foolishness in varying degrees. But it must be admitted that it is much more common today."

The same author wrote: "In every period of history God sets precursors who either act or think in the future. It is a great blessing for them to live in advance of their times, although it means that they live alone. Abraham had this good fortune, when he desired to see, and saw, the days of Christ more than 1,500 years before He came."[172]

To have within yourself, buried deep down, a clear view of all that must be done if the future is to be as Christ requires it to be — not merely in general, but in detail — and, despite misunderstandings, opposition, and contradiction, despite the inner distaste that all such antagonisms cause, to make hidden but effective preparations for the times that are to come: what a task! But what a glorious task!

A humorist said of a certain politician: "His misfortune is that he knows history; and so he lives in a cemetery." No, we must not despise the past; still less must we be ignorant of it. We must neglect nothing that may serve to give us a better understanding of the present, and of the organization that is

---

[172] Abbé de Tourville, *La piété confiante*, 163-164.

necessary for the future. Thank God that it is possible to know history and yet not live in a cemetery.

But more than the past, what we have to learn to know — so that we may make it as we want it to be — is the future. Let us never forget: we have to live — and we have to help other souls to live — a life without end, but a life that, on this earth, is set in a particular period of time. It is therefore of the highest importance that we should understand the times that are coming. Otherwise we run the risk of being out of date, incapable of influencing our own age, through lack of comprehensiveness, lack of foresight, or lack of adaptability. It may be that we shall die with our dream still buried in our hearts. But at least we shall have lived in a manner that makes life worth living.

Moreover, have we not the Church to help us in our imperfect comprehension of the future? She is believed to be exclusively preoccupied with Tradition. But she is just as much, if not more, preoccupied with the future. It is for us, her children, not to defy her directions when she gives them, but to accept them and, under her guidance, to march boldly ahead.

It may mean giving up some of our opinions, renouncing some of our dreams. Then let us bury ourselves by burying them carefully, and welcome the judgments, decisions, and directions of our Mother the Church.

Chapter Twelve

∞

Answer Christ's Call
to Be an Apostle

There are many who lament that the world fares ill today. Has there ever been a time when you think it fared well? Doubtless, sometimes it has fared better, sometimes worse; and you are at liberty to think that this is one of the "worse" moments. But what is the use of lamenting? It does no good. Rather let us say: if the world fares ill, then so much the more work for us to do if we want it to fare well.

Saving the world has never been an easy task. It was not easy for the Son of God. It was not easy for His Apostles. But He is with us. And that brings us back to the confidence of our beginning. Under such a leader, is there any limit to what soldiers may do, soldiers full of zeal and resolution, trained in His methods?

"I have overcome the world."[173] He does not speak of the future: "I will overcome the world." He uses the past tense: "I have overcome." One thing only is wanting to make this the present tense: your active, understanding, and intelligent collaboration. When all the "other Christs" have decided to help Christ, then redemption through Christ will be fully accomplished. Let us pray that apostles may come, and that they may be such as the world and God require them to be.

[173]John 16:33.

∞

Raoul Plus, S.J.
(1882-1958)

∞

Raoul Plus was born in Boulogne-sur-Mer, France, where he attended the Jesuit college. In 1899 he entered the Jesuit novitiate in Amiens and was ordained there. Because of laws that persecuted religious orders at that time, Fr. Plus had to leave France in 1901, and did not return from this exile for ten years, during which time he studied literature, philosophy, and theology in Belgium and Holland. He also taught courses in the field of humanities.

At the advent of World War I, Fr. Plus enlisted first as a soldier, and subsequently as chaplain, and later was awarded the *Croix de Guerre* and the *Medaille Militaire* for his heroism. It was during this time that he began to write, producing his first two books, which were followed by a host of works on various aspects of the spiritual life, and in particular, about the presence of Christ in the soul.

After the war, Fr. Plus taught religion at the Catholic Institute of Arts and Sciences in Lille and became a well-loved spiritual director for the students. During school vacations, he gave retreats for priests and seminarians and wrote several books concerning priests.

In his lifetime, Fr. Plus wrote more than forty books aimed at helping Catholics understand God's loving relationship with the soul. His words consistently stress the vital role of prayer in the spiritual life and seek to show how to live out important spiritual truths. His direct, practical style renders his works invaluable for those seeking to know Christ better and to develop a closer union with Him in their souls.

∞

Sophia Institute Press®